RUGBY LEAGUE JOURNAL ANNUAL 2008

RUGBY LEAGUE JOURNAL
PUBLISHING

First published in Great Britain in 2007 by
Rugby League Journal Publishing
P.O.Box 22, Egremont, Cumbria, CA23 3WA

ISBN 0-9548355-3-0
ISBN 13: 978-0-954835538

Edited and designed by Harry Edgar

Sales and Marketing by Ruth Edgar

Printed by Printexpress (Cumbria) Limited

Front cover pictures:
Main picture: Paul Wellens playing for Great Britain.
(Photograph by courtesy of Andrew Varley Picture Agency)
Inset pictures: Des Drummond, Kurt Sorensen and Neil Fox.
Frontispiece picture:
Jeff Stevenson and Keith Barnes leading out Great Britain and Australia at Central Park Wigan for the Ashes decider of 1959.
Jeff Stevenson passed away in October 2007.

RUGBY LEAGUE JOURNAL
PUBLISHING

P.O. Box 22, Egremont, Cumbria, CA23 3WA
E-Mail: rugbyleague.journal@virgin.net   Telephone: 01946 814249
www.rugbyleaguejournal.net

CONTENTS

BILLY BOSTON - one the best loved names in Rugby League, pictured as a young man in training with the Great Britain team in 1954. Billy made two Lions tours and played in two World Cup tournaments, and is remembered in this book as one of the finest to emerge from Tiger Bay.

Our thanks to all the photographers whose skills have provided so many fine images in this book. With so many old pictures from private collections it is often difficult to ascertain their origins, thus there has been no intention to breach anybody's copyright. Special thanks go to photographers: Eddie Whitham, who has unearthed some wonderful pictures from his archives; Andrew Varley, top Rugby League photographer and friend since the very early days of the former "Open Rugby" magazine and Mike McKenzie. Thanks also to: Andy Wheelwright, Sam Coulter, Ron Bailey, John Etty, Bill Nelson, John Chapman, John Donovan and all friends for their help in providing pictures.

6	League Tables - how they finished in 2007.
7	Paul Wellens - our player of the year.
8	On the line - the season in review.
10	Two great Wembley captains.
11	The Ashes 100th anniversary.
15	The very first Ashes Test remembered.
16	Alan Prescott on his epic Test of 1958.
19	How they brought the Ashes news back home.
20	The Munich disaster 50 years on.
21	Keiron Cunningham - the Super Saint.
22	When Wally Lewis came to Wakefield.
24	The Treasures of Tiger Bay.
26	Grounds fit for the Championship Final.
27	John Woods - always a Leigh champion.
28	The Odsal steps - a famous landmark.
30	Classic half-back partnerships.
32	Warrington's other Bevan - Welshman John.
33	Oh for the video ref for Cumbrians.
34	When 22,000 watched Blackpool Borough.
36	Early advert endorsements by Britain's best.
37	Club Nostalgia - files on all the old clubs.
70	Great Britain gallery - international portraits.
71	Trent Barrett and Wigan's timeless heroes.
72	David Seeds - tribute to a Whitehaven legend.
74	You've Got to Laugh - funny stories in R.L.
76	Cartoon time - Hull K.R.'s great season.
77	Enter the Time Tunnel - the past in pictures.
87	See the Rugby League Journal back-issues.
88	The next new thing in the world of League.
90	The Year in Australia.
92	The Year in New Zealand.
94	The Year in France.
96	The Year in Amateur Rugby League.
99	Robert Purdham - of Harlequins and England.
100	The World Cup in 2008.
102	All Great Britain's Ashes captains.
103	Great Britain international players register.
110	The other Great Britain international players.
111	Did you know? All the Quiz answers.
112	The Final Whistle.

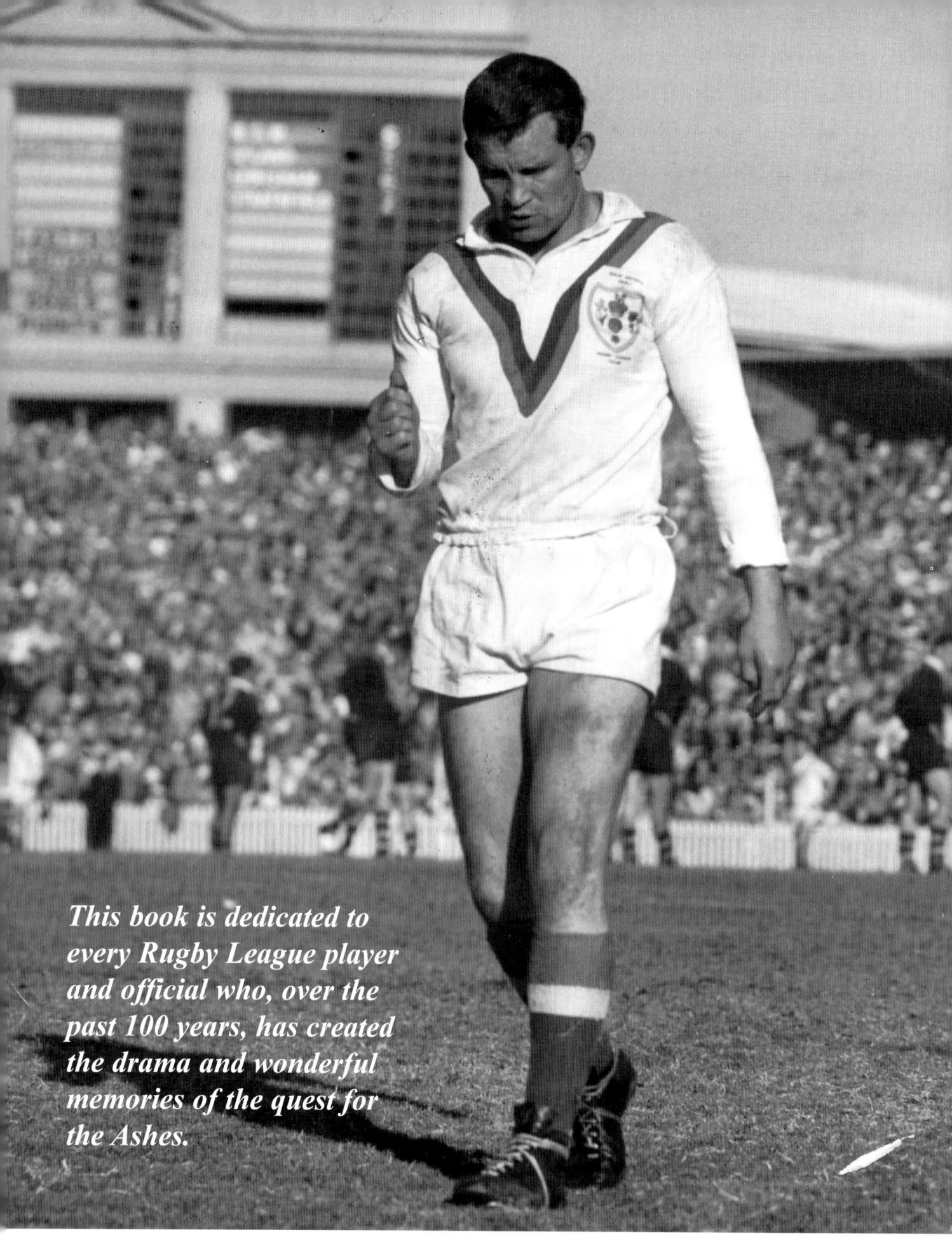

This book is dedicated to every Rugby League player and official who, over the past 100 years, has created the drama and wonderful memories of the quest for the Ashes.

MICK SULLIVAN - Great Britain's most capped international player - pictured taking the long walk off the Sydney Cricket Ground during the third Test of the sensational 1962 Ashes series.

Introduction

THIS is the fourth edition of the Annual produced by our quarterly magazine *"Rugby League Journal,"* and we welcome you to another huge collection of memorabilia and nostalgia. We describe our publication as being for fans who don't want to forget the game they used to know, and we hope all readers will enjoy their memories of the Rugby League players, teams and famous events of years gone by.

Our aim in producing this Annual is to be able to share with you some of the fascinating information, photographs and memorabilia we have collected which bring to life so many reminders of the old Rugby League game many of us grew up with. Unashamed nostalgia? - of course - but also an important exercise in helping ensure some of the admirable people who did so much to build Rugby League's wonderful heritage are not forgotten, and to encourage the younger generation of fans to learn more about the game's history.

In 2007 Rugby League celebrated the 100th anniversary of the birth of the international game created by the pioneering New Zealanders of 1907 led by Albert Baskerville. And in 2008, it will celebrate a similar anniversary of the visit to Britain by the very first Kangaroos touring team and with it the birth of the Ashes. In recognition of that landmark in the game's history, this Annual includes a section dedicated to memories of the Ashes and, in particular, the Kangaroos in Britain.

Compiling just a snapshot in retrospect of the Ashes provides a reminder of what an immense and dramatic story Rugby League created with its regular battles between Australia and old England (eventually to be known as Great Britain.) I have been fortunate enough to come to learn all about that story very well over many years of following Rugby League. From personal experience I can go back to the 1959 series, the last in which Great Britain were able to win the Ashes on home soil, and since then I've been around for every series right up to the dramatic moments of 2003 in which a desperately weakend Australia, inspired by Darren Lockyer and Brett Kimmorley, were able to maintain the green and golds' grip on the trophy in one of their nation's most heroic series victories.

Like so many fans of my generation, I was able to learn all about the dramas of previous Ashes contests by reading the reports of some of Rugby League's finest and most inspirational journalists. For the post War years, that was Eddie Waring, a man who accompanied the 1946 *"Indomitables"* and then every subsequent British touring team to Australia throughout the 1950s and '60s. And for in-depth coverage of a Lions tour, nothing could have been more extensive or informative than the regular reports cabled by Australian correspondents to Stanley Chadwick's *"Rugby League Review"* magazine in 1950.

Going back further to the pre-War years, knowledge of the Ashes story came from two of my great journalistic "heroes" of the past - Harry Sunderland and Tom Longworth - and I often wonder what they might have thought of the Rugby League world today which has so diminished the Ashes legacy. The last Ashes series was, as mentioned, in 2003, but we have not been able to stage a proper Kangaroo tour or Lions tour since the British game opted for a summer season in the mid-1990s.

In 1995, when Rugby League was being torn apart by the so-called "Super League war," the British official Maurice Lindsay - trying, one presumes, to justify what would happen to the hopes of staging future Test series between Great Britain and Australia - was infamously quoted as saying: *"I've never agreed with it being called the Ashes, anyway. The Ashes are in cricket."*

Those words still send a shiver down my spine everytime I re-read them. I have no idea when the next Ashes series might be planned, if one is planned at all. But for *"Rugby League Journal"* readers, the memories of the Ashes will remain, and their importance to the very fabric of the game we supported will never be underestimated.

2008 will also see a World Cup tournament staged in Australia as the Aussies celebrate the game's centenary in their country. The story of Rugby League's World Cup is another, like the Ashes, which holds such great fascinaton, most especially the sheer romance of Great Britain's triumphs in France in 1954 and 1972, led by inspirational figures like Dave Valentine and Clive Sullivan.

Valentine was a Scotsman and Sullivan a Welshman, and they both captained Great Britain to win the World Cup. Will we ever see a genuine Scot or Welshman in the Great Britain team again? In fact, supporters are going to have to get used to the idea of not having a Great Britain team at all to cheer on home soil, but England instead. It is part of the Rugby Football League's new policy that England should replace Great Britain except for "tours" to Australasia, which is something most people should be able to live with now that the British team in unlikely to have any non-English players in the forseeable future. The Irishman Brian Carney has left the game and nobody signs top players from Scotland or Wales anymore.

Rugby League is certainly a far less cosmopolitan sport than the one we knew in years gone by, unless you get excited by Scottish and Irish teams which are full of players who come from Lancashire, Yorkshire or Australia rather than Scotland or Ireland. On the other hand, we now have a French club, the Catalans, playing in the British competition and, in a remarkable achievement in 2007, reaching the Challenge Cup Final at Wembley.

So, you can see that nothing ever stands still in Rugby League, a game constantly evolving and never afraid to make innovative changes. With that in mind, we hope you enjoy all the memories contained in this Annual.

Harry Edgar (Editor)

HOW THEY FINISHED
FINAL LEAGUE TABLES 2007

SUPER LEAGUE

	P	W	D	L	For	Ag.	Diff	Pts
St. Helens	27	19	0	8	783	422	361	38
Leeds	27	18	1	8	747	487	260	37
Bradford*	27	17	1	9	778	560	218	33
Hull	27	14	2	11	573	553	20	30
Huddersfield	27	13	1	13	638	543	95	27
Wigan**	27	15	1	11	621	527	94	27
Warrington	27	13	0	14	693	736	-43	26
Wakefield Trin.	27	11	1	15	596	714	-118	23
Harlequins	27	10	3	14	495	636	-141	23
Catalans	27	10	1	16	570	685	-115	21
Hull K.R.	27	10	0	17	491	723	-232	20
Salford	27	6	1	20	475	874	-399	13

* 2 points deducted for salary cap breaches in 2006.
** 4 points deducted for salary cap breaches in 2006.

NATIONAL LEAGUE ONE

	P	W	D	L	B.P.	For	Ag.	Pts
Castleford	18	17	0	1	0	860	247	51
Widnes	18	16	0	2	2	740	220	50
Halifax	18	12	0	6	2	616	421	38
Whitehaven	18	11	0	7	5	474	342	38
Leigh	18	9	0	9	4	454	474	31
Sheffield	18	6	1	11	4	414	527	24
Dewsbury	18	5	0	13	6	346	527	21
Batley	18	5	1	12	2	372	645	19
Rochdale	18	3	0	15	1	302	700	10
Doncaster*	18	5	0	13	1	348	778	10

NATIONAL LEAGUE TWO

	P	W	D	L	B.P.	For	Ag.	Pts
Celtic Crus.	22	19	0	3	3	918	345	60
Featherstone	22	18	0	4	2	819	366	56
Barrow	22	17	0	5	4	769	387	55
Oldham	22	16	0	6	5	661	420	53
Workington T.	22	12	0	10	7	655	515	43
York	22	10	0	12	6	488	470	36
Swinton*	22	11	0	11	6	605	649	33
Hunslet	22	8	0	14	7	368	591	31
London Skol.	22	8	1	13	4	448	610	30
Keighley	22	6	1	15	4	407	692	24
Gateshead	22	6	0	16	3	381	822	21
Blackpool	22	0	0	22	6	332	984	6

* Denotes 6 points deducted for club in administration.

TRENT BARRETT - a star of the 2007 season for Wigan

DREAM TEAMS

The official "All Star" selections for the 2007 season named by the Rugby Football League in conjunction with their media associates - not this publication.

SUPER LEAGUE

1 - PAUL WELLENS (St.Helens); 2 - KEVIN PENNY (Warrington), 3 - ADAM MOGG (Catalans), 4 - JASON DEMETRIOU (Wakefield), 5 - SCOTT DONALD (Leeds); 6 - TRENT BARRETT (Wigan), 7 - ROB BURROW (Leeds); 8 - NICK FOZZARD (St.Helens), 9 - JAMES ROBY (St.Helens), 10 - JAMIE PEACOCK (Leeds), 11 - GARETH ELLIS (Leeds), 12 - GLEN MORRISON (Bradford), 13 - STEPHEN WILD (Huddersfield).

NATIONAL LEAGUE ONE

1 - SCOTT GRIX (Widnes); 2 - DAMIEN BLANCH (Widnes), 3 - MICHAEL SHENTON(Castleford), 4 - MICK NANYN (Widnes), 5 - DANNY MILLS (Sheffield Eagles); 6 - DENNIS MORAN (Widnes), 7 - DANNY BROUGH (Castleford); 8 - OLIVER WILKES (Widnes), 9 - SEAN PENKYWICZ (Halifax), 10 - MARK LEAFA (Castleford), 11 - RICHARD FLETCHER (Whitehaven), 12 - RYAN CLAYTON (Castleford), 13- BOB BESWICK (Widnes).

NATIONAL LEAGUE TWO

1 - TONY DUGGAN (Celtic Crusaders); 2 - DANNY KIRMOND (Featherstone), 3 - MARK DALLE-COURT (Celtic Crusaders), 4 - LIAM HARRISON (Barrow), 5 - AUSTEN AGGREY (London Skolars); 6 - NEIL RODEN (Oldham), 7 - JACE VAN DIJK (Celtic Crusaders); 8 - STUART DICKENS (Featherstone), 9 - NEIL BUDWORTH (Celtic Crusaders), 10 - ADAM SULLIVAN (York), 11 - NEALE WYATT (Celtic Crusaders), 12 - TOMMY HAUGHEY (Featherstone), 13 - DAMIEN QUINN (Celtic Crusaders).

TRIBUTE TO OUR FRONT COVER STAR - PAUL WELLENS

OUR *"Rugby League Journal Annual"* player of the year for 2007 is the St.Helens and Great Britain full-back Paul Wellens, who duly graces the front cover of this book.

After his wonderfully successful season in 2006 in which he won both the coveted "Man of Steel" award and the Harry Sunderland Trophy, Wellens continued where he left off in 2007. His remarkable consistency as the custodian of the successful St.Helens team - both as a superb last line of defence as well as one of his side's finest attacking footballers - makes him one of the most admired players in the modern game.

Indeed, in an era in which some others struggle to portray the kind of behaviour, demeanour and sportsmanship the game needs to see, Paul Wellens always stands out as a beacon of all that is good about Rugby League. Those with long memories can see Wellens as a player with good old fashioned values, proving himself to be an outstanding exponent of the modern game.

He added the Lance Todd trophy to his list of personal honours in 2007, and remains one of the greatest heroes of Saints fans who love seeing a local lad shine as one of the best in the game. Paul is maintaining a long list of popular and talented full-backs at Knowsley Road, among them such fine players as: Glyn Moses, Austin Rhodes, Frankie Barrow, Kel Coslett, Geoff Pimblett, Gary Connolly, Phil Veivers and Steve Prescott.

Originally a half-back, Wellens made his first-team debut for St.Helens when he came on at scrum-half as a substitute for Sean Long. "I just felt so privileged to be in the first team, I would have played anywhere in any position for Saints," says Paul. "But with Sean Long making the half-back position his own I eventually switched positions to full-back and from the year 2000 I never looked back. I have to pinch myself sometimes to remind myself that I'm playing for the club that I supported from the terraces as a schoolboy. Playing for St.Helens is like a dream come true for me."

2007

PUTTING IT ON THE LINE - THE 2007 SEASON IN REVIEW

LEEDS and St.Helens were the big winners of British Rugby League in the 2007 season as the Super League continued to enjoy booming crowds and exciting competition, includng a thrilling top-six play-off series.

At numerous stages during the season, many pundits wondered whether anyone could halt the Saints' domination of the major trophies as they looked on course for a second successive "treble" of the Super League championship, league leaders' trophy and Challenge Cup. But St.Helens were to fall at the final hurdle thanks to a stunning display by Leeds in the Grand Final at Old Trafford.

A crowd of 71,352 gathered in Manchester on October 13th, to see Leeds produce an outstanding performance on both attack and defence to take the Grand Final by an eventual margin of 33-6 over St.Helens. Majestically led by Kevin Sinfield, pepped up by the jack-in-a-box scrum-half Rob Burrow, and with the mighty Jamie Peacock leading his pack forward, Leeds were awesome and Saints - so used to being top dog - had no answer on the night.

Such a triumph in taking the Championship was a fitting send-off from Headingley for the departing coach Tony Smith, who moved on to a position as full-time head coach of the Great Britain, and later England, national teams.

KEVIN SINFIELD captained Leeds to glory in the Super League Grand Final of 2007.

St.Helens had to satisfy themselves with victories earlier in the season which had seen them kick off by beating the Australian champions, Brisbane Broncos, to claim the World Club Challenge. Saints then went on to become the first team to lift the Challenge Cup at the new Wembley Stadium. The Cup Final, played on August 25th, turned up one of the greatest fairy-stories the game has seen in recent times when the French-based side, the Catalan Dragons, lined up against St.Helens.

Cup Final returns to Wembley

Inspired by their talisman captain, the New Zealander Stacey Jones, the Catalans caused a massive upset by knocking Wigan out in the semi-final (after earlier winning at Hull in the quarter-final) to win a Wembley place in only their second season as a full-time professional club playing in the Super League. The fairy-story could not continue in the new stadium in front of 84,241 people - which was the biggest attendance any French rugby team (of either code) has ever played in front of - as St.Helens live up to their favourites tag to win 30-8.

Local boy Keiron Cunningham lifted the Cup for the Saints after a match that was low on quality compared to the Super League Grand Final that followed, and was also marred by the refereeing controversies that have become such a part and parcel of the Super League. As well as those referees, the 2007 season also had other controversial issues to deal with, not least, breaches of the Salary Cap which left Wigan shamed and docked four points in the championship table. And the city of Hull found itself wrapped up in one of the most controversial transfer stories since the day Jonty Parkin paid Wakefield Trinity his own fee and negiotated a deal with Hull Kingston Rovers, when Paul Cooke opted to walk out on Hull F.C. and cross to the east of the city. The "Robins" were again the beneficiaries.

In fact the presence of newly promoted Hull K.R. in the Super League had much to do with the competition posting a 13.7 percent increase in attendances on the previous year. The "Robins" ensured their neighbours Hull got two derby sell-out crowds at the K.C. Stadium and their travelling support to all other grounds was significantly bigger than numerous other clubs, not least on the night they provided Salford with their biggest home crowd of the season as the relegation battle reached its zenith.

Those impressive crowd figures saw top club Leeds record an average home league attendance of 17,558 -

which was the highest average at Headingley since the Second World War - in fact every club in the Super League posted an increase in their average attendances with the exception of St.Helens and the Harlequins.

The outstanding talent of Saints' 21-year-old James Roby was honoured when he was named the *Man of Steel* as the Super League's outstanding player in 2007. Roby had a big impact on the St.Helens success in the Challenge Cup Final, coming off the substitutes' bench - as he invariably does - to score the first try at the new Wembley. As a prototype of the modern 17-man game, young Roby has emerged as a wonderfully talented example of the way the game is played in 2007. One game he did actually start in the number nine shirt was for Great Britain in their sole in-season international of 2007, in which they beat France 42-14 at Headingley. Adrian Morley had been a surprise choice to captain Great Britain for the first time.

Salford relegated to National League

Salford, after all their success and optimism of the previous year, were the team who finished in the relegation position and will play 2008 in the National League One. For the Red Devils, eager to secure a long-term future in the Super League at a new stadium, that brings worrying times - as it will for many clubs in the National League who ponder what the future holds for them once the drawbridge on promotion/relegation is pulled up from 2009.

One club happy not to be worrying about that now is Castleford who achieved their immediate return to the elite by winning the National League One title, thrashing their closest rivals Widnes 42-10 in the Grand Final. The decision to move that game to the prestigious venue of Headingley was fully justified when a record crowd of 20,814 turned out to see Cas' storm home.

Casleford and Widnes continued to operate as full-time professional teams playing in a basically semi-pro league, so it was no surprise that they finished clear of all their competitors, although Widnes did lose away at Halifax and twice needed some large doses of good fortune as they struggled to overcome Whitehaven both home and away. But the game's folly of causing such a wide gap between Super League and the rest was painfully illustrated by the news that Widnes, just 24 hours after losing to Castleford in the Grand Final and knowing they would not get promotion, went into administration and, within hours, saw many of their players leave for other clubs.

Earlier in the season, similar craziness was seen at Doncaster who also went into meltdown when reality dawned after what appeared to be a pretty embarrassing series of events. Happily, the Dons were rescued by local fans and began the long road back to credibility, despite being relegated along with Rocndale Hornets. In a pleasing reversal of recent trends, both promoted teams - Dewsbury and Sheffield Eagles - managed to prosper in the higher levels of National League One.

Champions of National League Two were the Celtic Crusaders, in only their second season in the league and providing a fascinating development for the game into

JAMES ROBY - the St.Helens star was the "Man of Steel" for the 2007 season.

South Wales. The Bridgend-based club appeared not to have any problems with the salary cap or import player quotas and import coaching restrictions that hampered other National League clubs, and responded by playing extremely entertaining and successful rugby which deserved far bigger crowds than they managed to muster at the Brewery Field. With a host of further professional recruits already announced for 2008, the Celtic Crusaders are likely to be a force in National League One.

They will be joined there by Featherstone Rovers who overcame Oldham 24-6 in their play-off Final, played as a curtain-raiser to the Castleford-Widnes Grand Final at Headingley.

With the arrival of a "licence" system for membership of the Super League in 2009, the time will be perfect for a re-organisation of the National League as the forlorn hope for many of *"getting into t'Super League"* will be formally brought to a close by the end of the current promotion and relegation system. It is essential that the Rugby Football League finds a way to ensure it has a vibrant second tier of semi-professional clubs and thus manages to re-energise those clubs in areas where interest in the game has always been part of the community but where active support has been allowed to wither as more and more have been made to feel alienated.

TWO GREAT WEMBLEY CAPTAINS - DEREK TURNER & ERNEST WARD

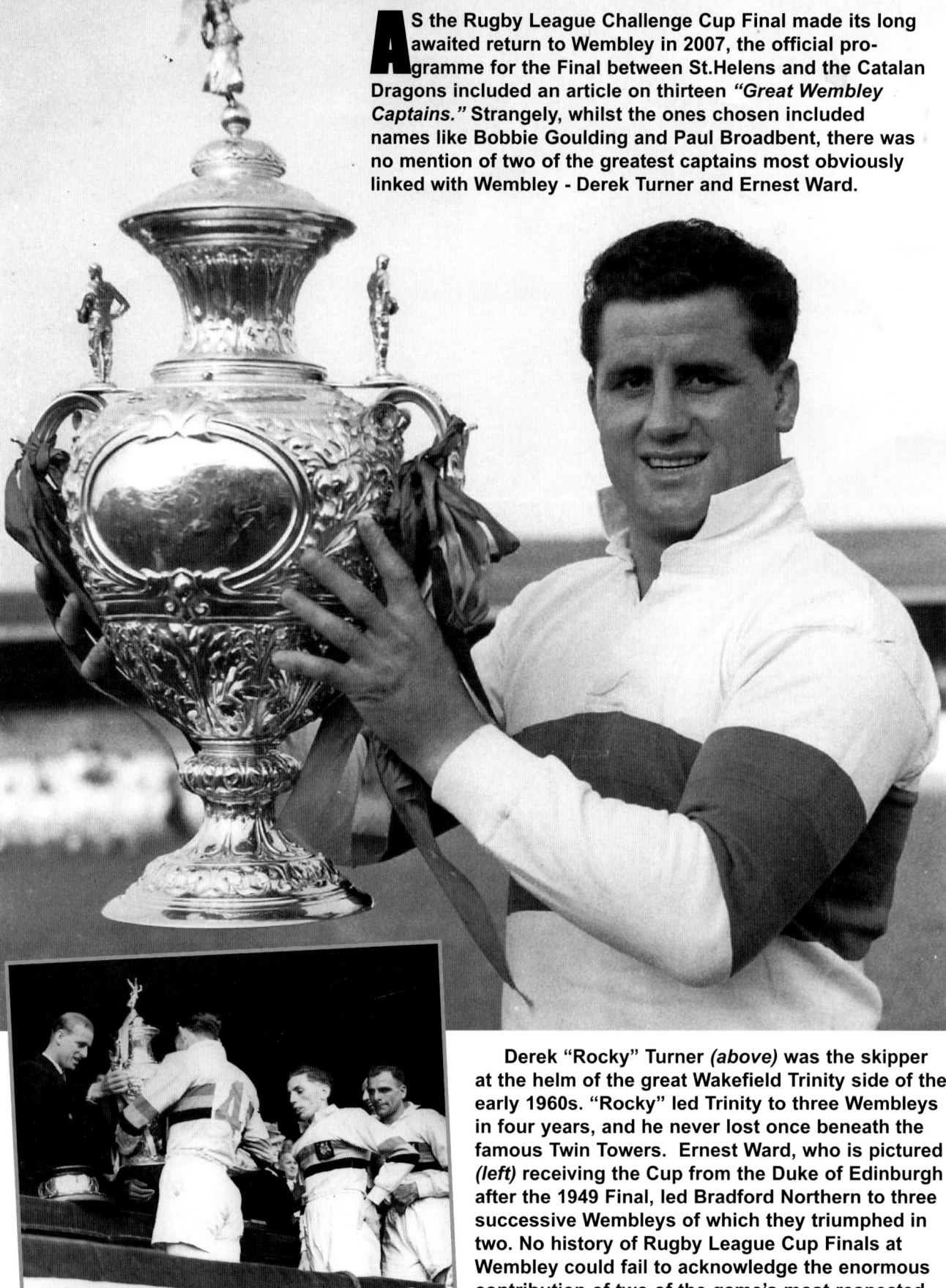

As the Rugby League Challenge Cup Final made its long awaited return to Wembley in 2007, the official programme for the Final between St.Helens and the Catalan Dragons included an article on thirteen *"Great Wembley Captains."* Strangely, whilst the ones chosen included names like Bobbie Goulding and Paul Broadbent, there was no mention of two of the greatest captains most obviously linked with Wembley - Derek Turner and Ernest Ward.

Derek "Rocky" Turner *(above)* was the skipper at the helm of the great Wakefield Trinity side of the early 1960s. "Rocky" led Trinity to three Wembleys in four years, and he never lost once beneath the famous Twin Towers. Ernest Ward, who is pictured *(left)* receiving the Cup from the Duke of Edinburgh after the 1949 Final, led Bradford Northern to three successive Wembleys of which they triumphed in two. No history of Rugby League Cup Finals at Wembley could fail to acknowledge the enormous contribution of two of the game's most respected captains - Derek Turner and Ernest Ward.

The Ashes - 100th Anniversary

In 2008 Rugby League celebrates the 100th Anniversary of the birth of the Ashes

Photo by EDDIE WHITHAM

How we'll always remember the excitement of the arrival of a Kangaroo touring team - and this was one of the best, the 1967 Australian side led by Reg Gasnier and including some of the Aussies' all-time greats, pictured before the opening match of their tour at Warrington. Left to right, *(Standing):* Kevin Goldspink, Elton Rasmussen, Noel Kelly, Ron Lynch, Ken Irvine, Graeme Langlands. *(Seated):* Johnny King, Dennis Manteit, Reg Gasnier (captain), Johnny Raper, Johnny Gleeson. *(In front):* Billy Smith, Les Johns.

(Left) DES DRUMMOND, one of Great Britain's best in the 1980s, pictured playing in Australia on the 1984 Lions tour.

12

The Ashes - 100th Anniversary

The memorable saga of Kangaroo tours

THE landmark of the 100th Anniversary of the birth of the Ashes also means the century milestone for the story of Kangaroo tours. Whist much of the Ashes drama has centred around Lions tours down-under, the adventures of Australian touring teams to the "mother country" have been an equally memorable saga.

For every Aussie Rugby League player the dream of becoming a Kangaroo has always been the ultimate. And, it should be remembered, that until recently when the term "Kangaroo" became just a marketing slogan, that honour was only bestowed on those Australians who were selected for a tour to Britain (and, since 1937, also to France.) Playing in Test matches at home, or on tour in New Zealand, did not carry the accolade of being a "Kangaroo" - that belonged exclusively to those who had toured Europe.

British fans of various generations will always have their own vivid memories of seeing Kangaroo touring teams and the special mystique they used to bring to the game in England every four years. The early post-War tours brought us Clive Churchill, the man they called *"The Little Master"* - and many will recall the impact made by the brilliant Reg Gasnier in 1959. Gasnier returned in 1963 and '67, along with Langlands and Raper, and then in 1982 everything changed as a new breed swept through the British game in the guise of Max Krilich's *"Invincibles."*

(Above) Two of the best known figures as Ashes captains - Keith Barnes and Eric Ashton - lead their countries out at Station Road in 1959.
(Left) The Ashes trophy presented for the first time in 1946 to the winning British team.

(Pictured, right) Kangaroos on tour in England.
(Above) On board the tour bus with the 1959 Aussies, including the young Reg Gasnier at the front and Noel Kelly at the back.
(Below) The Australian war-dance performed in 1948 before the opening game of the tour at Huddersfield. The last Aussie team to perform the war-dance was the 1967 Kangaroos.

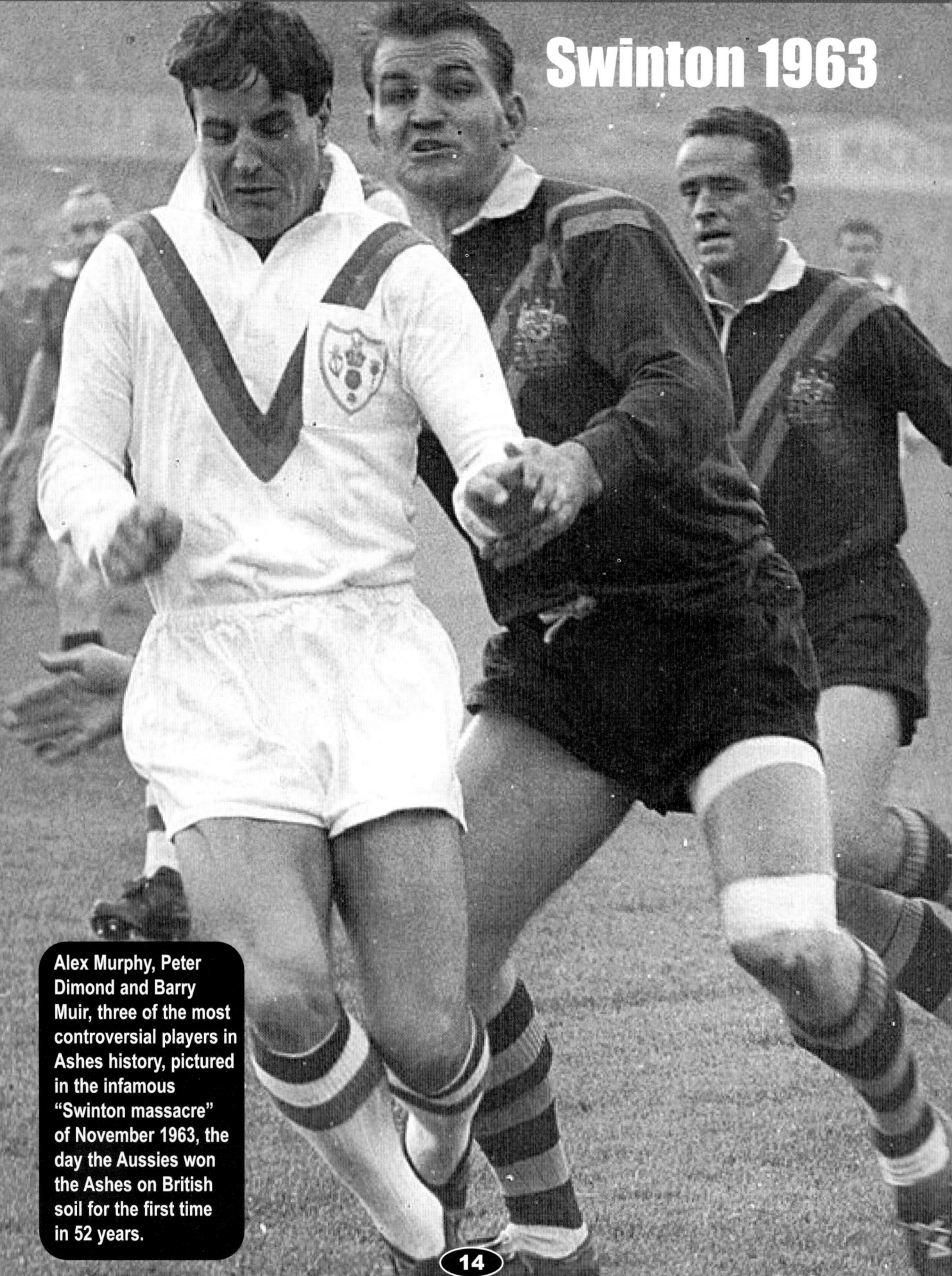

The Ashes - 100th Anniversary

Swinton 1963

Alex Murphy, Peter Dimond and Barry Muir, three of the most controversial players in Ashes history, pictured in the infamous "Swinton massacre" of November 1963, the day the Aussies won the Ashes on British soil for the first time in 52 years.

The Ashes - 100th Anniversary

Very first Ashes Test was a draw in London

THE Ashes tradition in Rugby League was born one hundred years ago in 1908. Hot on the heels of the pioneering first tour by A. H. Baskerville and his New Zealand team - the "All Golds" - in the previous season, the Northern Union in England were delighted to welcome the first Kangaroos touring team from Australia in 1908-1909.

The Aussies had already played no less than 19 games on their tour before they arrived at the first Test match on 12th December, 1908. This very first Anglo-Australian Test match was played at the Park Royal stadium in London, home of the Queens Park Rangers association football club - and the birth of what was to become such a wonderful Ashes tradition was celebrated with a 22-all draw in what was reported as a highly entertaining match.

The honour of scoring the very first Ashes points went to Australia's captain "Dally" Messenger who kicked a penalty-goal to open the scoring; and the first Ashes try was scored by the British half-back Johnny Thomas.

One of the game's immortals, Billy Batten, was the second man to score a try as the home country established a half-time lead of 14-5. But a second-half comeback by the Australians, inspired by the masterful Messenger, put them in front and it needed a very late penalty-goal, kicked by stand-off Ernie Brooks, to level the scores and see this historic match finish as a draw.

Compared to a sport that has become so parochial 100 years later, it is fascinating to see the Northern Union's pioneering spirit in their choice of venues for that very first Ashes series. The opening Test at Park Royal proved to be a flop at the gate when only 2,000 spectators turned up and provided receipts of just £70; in contrast - less than 12 months earlier - 15,000 people had attended a Test against the New Zealanders staged by the Northern Union at Chelsea's Stamford Bridge ground.

JOHNNY THOMAS
The first man to score a try in the history of Ashes Test matches.

(Above) The first Kangaroos touring team in 1908.

The first Ashes series of 1908-09 was completed with further Tests at Newcastle's St.James' Park and Villa Park in Birmingham, which drew much more encouraging crowds of 22,000 and 9,000 respectively and saw the British win the series with two victories, 15-5 and 6-5. In both those successful games against the Australians, Britain were captained by Salford's Cumbrian centre Jim "Jumbo" Lomas, who became the first man to lead his country to victory in an Ashes series, although - back then - there was no Ashes trophy to be presented to the winners. That was to come in the years that followed.

THE VERY FIRST ASHES TEST MATCH

12th December, 1908 - at Park Royal, London
GREAT BRITAIN 22 - AUSTRALIA 22

Full-back
H. GIFFORD (Barrow)
Threequarters
G. TYSON (Oldham)
G. DICKENSON (Warrington)
T.B. JENKINS (Wigan) *Capt.*
W. BATTEN (Hunslet)
Half-backs
E. BROOKS (Warrington)
J. THOMAS (Wigan)
Forwards
A. ROBINSON (Halifax)
A. SMITH (Oldham)
W.H. LONGWORTH (Oldham)
W. JUKES (Hunslet)
J.W. HIGSON (Hunslet)
A. MANN (Bradford)

Full-back
M. BOLEWSKI (Bundaberg)
Threequarters
W.G. HEIDKE (Bundaberg)
S.P. DEANE (Norths)
J.DEVEREAUX (Norths)
H.H. MESSENGER (Easts)
Half-backs
A. HALLOWAY (Easts)
A. BUTLER (Souths)
Forwards
P. WALSH (Newcastle)
E.J. COURTNEY (Newtown)
S.C. PEARCE (Easts)
A. BURDON (Glebe)
J. ABERCROMBIE (Wests)
L. O'MALLEY (Easts)

Referee: Mr. J. H. SMITH (Widnes)

The Ashes - 100th Anniversary

Alan Prescott and his British heroes of 1958

Anglo-Australian Test series were born 100 years ago, but in 2008 Rugby League will celebrate the 50th anniversary of one of the truly epic moments in Ashes history.

It will be half a century on from 1958 when Great Britain captain Alan Prescott lead his Lions team to victory in one of the greatest Test triumphs of all time. After losing the first Test to Australia in Sydney, to save the series Great Britain had to win the second which was played at the Brisbane Exhibition Ground on 5th July, 1958. Prop-forward Prescott broke his arm just four minutes into the game - but, in those days of no substitutes, he stayed on the field for the full 80 minutes to inspire his injury ravaged team to glorious victory. It was a display of incredible courage which should never be forgotten. Here we re-live the story of that game in the words of Alan Prescott himself, in an interview recorded with him in 1983 - 25 years on from his "Brisbane epic."

(Pictured, right) Prescott, his broken arm in a sling, holds the Ashes trophy as he is carried on a lap of honour round the Sydney Cricket Ground after victory in the 1958 third Test. His team-mates are, *left to right:* manager Tom Mitchell, Alan Davies, Ike Southward, Vince Karalius, Mick Sullivan, Phil Jackson, Eric Fraser and Johnny Whiteley.

"I can't go off, we've got to win" - said skipper Prescott

"I knew right away when I broke my arm that day in 1958. I could always remember the moment clearly -

I tackled Australia's acting half-back Rex Mossop and my arm struck his head and smashed. It went numb and I knew it was broken. I thought to myself 'you can't go off, this Test match has got to be won.'

I was on that field in Brisbane wondering if I could do any permanent damage when the words of the late, great Jim Sullivan came to me. Jim once said to me, if you are only on the field getting in the way then someone has got to beat you. Always stand and face the opposition, never turn your back. These words renewed my determination. I knew I had to stay on.

The first person I told about the injury was our hooker Tommy Harris. In the fourth scrum Harris shouted to me: 'Come on Alan the scrum's loose.' I replied: 'Sorry Tom, I've broken my arm.' Then Jim Challinor hurt himself when he collided with the corner flag as he scored. 'I'll have to go off,' Jim said to me and I replied: 'You're joking - I've got a broken arm and you want to go off!'

Then Dave Bolton broke his collar bone and had to come off and Eric Fraser burst a blood vessel in his arm. Vinty Karalius bruised his spine and was in a lot of pain. So, although we were winning 10-2 at half-time, the dressing-room was quiet - it should have been buzzing because we were in front, but there were so many injured players

The Ashes - 100th Anniversary

that concern took over about how we could manage in the second-half. Only Alex Muprhy stayed relaxed, confident as ever as he stood in front of a mirror combing his brylcreamed hair - that's arrogance for you, but he was having a storming game.

The Australian doctor had a look at my arm and advised me to stay off the field, warning that if I continued I could do permanent damage. But I told our team manager, Tom Mitchell: 'I just can't go off - we'd be two men short and we've got to win.' It was the look on the other players' faces that kept me going. The other lads were watching for my reaction - they were ready for the second-half despite being in pain. This made me feel very proud and I stood up and shouted: 'come on lads, let's go and destroy these Aussies.'

I may have played a big part, but every player was magnificent that day. We battled through and were overjoyed when we won 25-18. I ran to Tom Mitchell and screamed 'we've done it.' It was then, however, that I started to realise how bad my arm was and I became anxious - facing 13 Australians with a broken arm didn't bother me, but the thought of an operating table frightened me to death.

When I discovered the nature of the break I knew we needed a mircacle to battle through - well the miracle came in the shape of a tremendous surge of patriotic feeling by the players. They did their country proud. It was a moving occasion.

Although I couldn't play in the third and deciding Test match, I had every confidence in the players. When the team includes such as Southward, Sullivan, Murphy, Huddart, Whiteley and Karalius, you are talking class with a capital C. They won 40-17 and despite my broken arm I was carried around the ground in Sydney with the Ashes - it was the highlight of my career."

Alan Prescott

ALAN PRESCOTT
"They made me feel proud"

G.B.'s glory in 1970

Great Britain's last taste of Ashes glory came in 1970 when, after losing the first Test in Brisbane, they stormed back to win the remaining two Tests at the Sydney Cricket Ground. In the picture *(above)* **Doug Laughton** is in possession for the Lions in the epic third Test win of 1970 with, in the background, forwards Tony Fisher, Malcolm Reilly and Cliff Watson from a very formidable British pack. It was Laughton who set up the try for Roger Millward which sealed victory in this match and the Ashes. None of us, especially Britain's captain in 1970 Frank Myler, could have predicted that almost 40 years later we would still be waiting to win the Ashes again.

The Ashes - 100th Anniversary

The end of Britain's thirty years of Ashes dominance

IT was a moment Australian Rugby League will never forget - the day thirty consecutive years of suffering the pain of defeat in the Ashes was finally relieved. It came on the Saturday afternoon of 22nd July, 1950, as the Aussies beat Great Britain 5-2 to clinch their first series win against the "mother country" since 1920.

Those three decades of Ashes domination by the British would be impossible to comprehend by today's followers of the game who have known nothing but Australia's stranglehold on the Ashes trophy for the past 34 years. But all things can come to an end in sport, and back then the Aussies always knew that every four years they would get a chance to challenge the British on home turf - not that there was too much turf at the Sydney Cricket on that famous day in 1950, as the Cricket Ground was turned into a morass of mud in many parts after a long spell of terrible weather on Australia's east coast.

The key moment came with 15 minutes left on the clock as Australia's lanky winger Ron Roberts got on the end of a sweeping backline move to sprint for the corner and slide over on the greasy surface to score the most famous try in the history of Australian Rugby League.

"I'd dropped a few passes that day because the ball was like a bar of soap," Roberts recalled many years later,

How the crowd at the Sydney Cricket Ground saw Ron Roberts score the most famous try in Australian Rugby League history and clinch the Ashes in 1950. *(Inset)* A closer view as the winger Roberts (wearing number 9 as wingers still did in Australia in those days) dives over to score.

"but I caught the one that mattered and scored the try." Aussie captain Clive Churchill was carried shoulder high by deliriously happy spectators who had queued through the night in torrential rain to be ready for when the gates opened at 7 am - such was the public interest in the Test that offered Australia the chance of breaking their Ashes drought. Those who were there would never forget it, but two years later Great Britain would reclaim the Ashes.

The Ashes - 100th Anniversary

A far cry from today's live television coverage beamed back home to the U.K. by satellite. Gus Risman broadcasts on the radio at the Sydney Cricket Ground after England's (Great Britain's) victory over Australia in the third Test in 1936 had clinched the Ashes - conducting the interview and holding the microphone is tour manager Robert Anderton. Others in the picture are, left to right: Nat Silcock, Walter Popllewell (manager), Emlyn Jenkins, Barney Hudson and Harry Beverley.

Bringing Ashes news to the folks back home

THE British boys far away in Australia; or the Kangaroos travelling to the "Mother Country" - the battles for the Ashes have always been fought on the other side of the world for one of the competing teams.

So far from home, it was essential that news of their exploits should be got back to the friends, families and all the game's supporters in their native land. Today, of course, in the age of satellite television and now the internet, sports fans just take it for granted that they can have live coverage of their teams playing overseas. Without getting up from the armchair in your living-room, you can press a remote-control and immediately be transported to a football stadium in Australia.

The story of how the media coverage of British Rugby League tours down-under to Australasia evolved over the near century since their first tour there in 1910, would make a fascinating study in itself. Before radio and transcontinental telephone lines came on the scene, written reports had to be sent home by cable. Press reporters did not accompany the early tours and the British newspapers were reliant on local Australian correspondents or the tour managers to furnish them with reports. Of the latter, the most media savvy of all the managers was Robert (Bob) Anderton of Warrington, who accompanied both the 1932 and 1936 Lions as they brought home the Ashes. Mr.

Anderton wrote reports for the newspapers and also took extensive cine films of the Test matches which were shown to fascinated audiences on his return to blighty.

It was the first tour after World War Two, the famous *"Indomitables,"* which saw the start in earnest of members of the press accompanying the British team to Australia. Eddie Waring led the way as one of three reporters with that 1946 team, and Eddie wrote a book about his experiences on the tour when he got home. Eddie then went on to take pride in becoming the only British press man to accompany every single post-War British tour down-under, a record he kept right up to the 1970 tour. As well as writing in the *"Sunday Pictorial"* he would also bring home the films of the Test matches which proved such a hit with the fans at home in his very popular film-shows around the country.

The BBC first sent their own radio correspondent with a Rugby League team to Australia in 1979, when Keith Macklin was a part of one of the biggest-ever press corps to go on tour. And the BBC's first live television coverage came in 1988, in the north of England only - Ray French added his comments to the Australian Channel Nine team; meanwhile BBC Radio had live commentary on those Ashes Tests provided by a certain Eddie Hemmings and Mike Stephenson - a pointer of things to come!

Station Road, Swinton - 8th February 1958

50 YEARS ON

OF all the sporting anniversaries to be commemorated in 2008, it is likely that none will draw more attention and be more poignant than the one that will mark the passsing of 50 years since the Munich air disaster which wiped out some of our country's finest footballing talent with the Manchester United team.

The United team, in manager Matt Busby's quest for the European Cup, had played a key quarter-final match in Belgrade against Red Star, and were on their way home to Manchester. But, the next day, 6th February, 1958, their aeroplane crashed trying to take off in a blizzard after refuelling at Munich. The death toll included eight players, two club officials, eight journalists and three others.

It was only natural that the effects of the tragedy were to be most strongly felt in the North West of England. The picture *(above)* shows the scene two days later at Manchester's most famous Rugby League ground, Station Road, as the players of Swinton and Featherstone Rovers lined up to pay their respects with a minute's silence. Note that the Swinton team were wearing black arm-bands as they remembered their fellow sportsmen from their city.

The eight newspaper men lost in the Munich tragedy were among Deansgate's finest, and several of them had - four years earlier - covered the first Rugby League World Cup tournament in France. The one journalist to survive was Frank Taylor, a native Barrowvian, who had been another to cover the Rugby League World Cup in 1954 and who, in later years, always remembered that adventure with Dave Valentine's British Rugby league team as one of his most enjoyable times in sports reporting.

Frank, who wrote for the *"News Chronicle and Daily Dispatch"* where he was a colleague of the eminent Rugby League correspondent Tom Longworth, had to endure a long struggle to overcome the injuries he sustained in the plane crash in which he lost so many friends and colleagues - but he never overcame the emotional scars. His legacy is the enormously moving personal story of that black day in British sport, a book entitled *"The Day A Team Died,"* first published in 1960 and re-printed several times since. For many years after, Frank Taylor was always a regular in the Wembley press-box at the Rugby League Challenge Cup Final. On a much happier note, 2008 will also mark the 50th anniversary of the famous Brisbane Test match of 1958 - Alan Prescott's epic.

SUPER SAINT

IN the modern era of Super League, no player has been at the very top of the British game for longer than St.Helens hooker Keiron Cunningham.

Keiron was there at the birth of Super League, and he's still there now after starring for more than 12 years in its most successful team - the Saints. He was a young starlet in the St.Helens team that won the double in 1996 and thus became the very first European Super League Champions; and he was their most dominant force of experience and power as the Saints continued to win doubles over a decade later.

Fittingly, Cunningham - as the only survivor still playing at Knowsley Road from the Saints team that won at Wembley in 1996 and 1997- was captain as they returned to the new Wembley in 2007. And no skipper was ever more proud to lift the Challenge Cup for his local team.

Photo by ANDREW VARLEY Picture Agency

WHEN WALLY CAME TO WAKEFIELD

Worshipping at the feet of the King? Warrington's Phil Ford finds himself on his knees before Wally Lewis but the great Australian of Wakefield Trinity had already got his pass away. The Trinity player on the left is Nigel Stephenson and the referee is Geoff Berry, this in one of the ten games Wally played for Wakefield back in 1983-84. *PHOTO by EDDIE WHITHAM.*

FOR years in the 1980s and early '90s Wakefield Trinity supporters could enjoy a "Fanzine" publication which went by the unforgettable name of *"Wally Lewis Is Coming."*

It was inspired by the hope of Trinity fans - a forlorn hope as things turned out - that the great Australian player who graced their club's colours during a guest spell in the 1983-84 season would return to play for Wakefield again. Trinity badly needed the inspiration they had seen provided by one of the game's all-time greats, and it seemed like at the start of every new season after 1984 that the directors at Belle Vue would try to rally their supporters by proclaiming in the press that Wally Lewis *is* coming back.

Of course, Wally never did come back to Wakefield. Yet the impact he made on Trinity was so dramatic that it is still talked about to this day - all of 24 years later. And this despite the fact that Wally Lewis only ever played TEN games for Wakefield Trinity.

After the famous tour by the 1982 *"Invincibles,"* Wally had returned to England in the Autumn of 1983 as captain of the Queensland state team which made a three-match tour. That increased his standing even further and, as the Anglo-Australian transfers ban was finally lifted in November, 1983 after six years in place, the floodgates were about to open as all the leading English clubs rushed to recruit Aussie stars to play over here in their off-season.

It was a bit of a surprise when Wakefield persuaded Wally to join them as Trinity were not among the top sides and were struggling in the relegation zone. But the lure of the then incredible terms of £1,000 per match (sponsored by a wealthy club supporter) was enough to tempt Lewis away from the sunshine of Queensland to come to the north of England in the depth of winter.

Wally flew out of Brisbane on 2nd December, 1983, the day after his 24th birthday, and the following day was driven straight from the airport to Wakefield's Belle Vue

Wally Lewis being sent off by referee Peter Massey in 1984.

More Aussie "Invincibles" came to play as guests

THE impact made on British Rugby League by the 1982 Australian touring team was immense. The Kangaroo side known as the "Invincibles" not only rocked our game to its foundations by hammering Great Britain in all three Tests, several of its players came back to these shores to play for English clubs and made an enormous impact in improving and popularising the game.

The lifting of the Anglo-Australian transfers ban at the end of 1983 saw the floodgates begin to open for Aussie players coming to England. And, of course, in those days before the British game backed itself into a corner by opting to play in a "summer" season, the way was open for top Australian players to play as guests and still return to their home clubs without missing any of the Aussie season.

As well as Wally Lewis at Wakefield, none made a bigger impact than the 1982 Kangaroo half-backs, Brett Kenny and Peter Sterling - team-mates at Parramatta but on opposing sides in the epic 1985 Wembley Final between Wigan and Hull. At the same time Mal Meninga was starring for St.Helens and, soon after, Leeds recruited the "Guru" himself, winger Eric Grothe. They were all guests made mighty welcome.

ground where Trinity coach, Derek "Rocky" Turner, was waiting to introduce him to his new colleagues. The tale of those introductions has become a part of Rugby League folklore when, apparently, several Trinity players refused to shake Wally's hand as they were jealous of his reported £1,000 a match fee. Wakefield captain Nigel Stephenson did his best to placate matters, reassuring Wally that everything would be okay and, no doubt, recognising that the Aussie's influence on the team's ability to win games was going to be nothing but positive.

Jet-lag was not an issue for Wally Lewis as he made his debut for Wakefield at Belle Vue two days after leaving Brisbane airport, on 4th December, 1983, against a Hull team which included another newly arrived Kangaroo star Peter Sterling. Over 8,000 fans turned out, their biggest crowd for a league match at Belle Vue for ten years and more than double their usual figure before Wally's arrival. His impact on the Trinity team was immediate and it soon became apparent that Wally's magical skills were carrying the side. The fans turned out in their thousands to see Lewis play - when he played his last game for Wakefield away at Thrum Hall in the Challenge Cup, the Halifax club actually paid for adverts on Yorkshire Television urging people to come and *"see the great Wally Lewis."* These were echoes of those Rugby League legendary stories from many years before about Hull putting up posters proclaiming *"Batten will play,"* in the knowledge this would draw thousands of fans to see the famous Billy Batten in action.

During his stay in Wakefield, Wally lodged at the Royal Oak pub as a guest of Brian Briggs, the former Trinity and Great Britain second-row-forward. In the ten memorable games he played in the white, red and blue, Wally led Wakefield to five wins and also suffered the wrath of referee Peter Massey who sent him off in one match for, allegedly, giving dissent. That was Wally, always with plenty to say, but one of the greatest footballers the game has seen - for a career that only lasted ten games with them, the mark he made on Wakefield was unforgettable.

BRETT KENNY and PETER STERLING - the two great Australians who found themselves on opposite sides for Wigan and Hull in the unforgettable 1985 Wembley Final.

The Treasures of TIGER BAY

THE action photograph you see above was taken during the 1961 Challenge Cup semi-final between Wigan and Halifax played before over 35,000 spectators at Swinton's Station Road ground. It shows the unmistakable figure of **Billy Boston** powering down the wing as the Halifax defence does its best to stop him. The Halifax man covering across on the inside is winger **Johnny Freeman.**

Boston and Freeman - two of the household names of the game in an era of prolific try-scoring wingers who were huge heroes in towns across the north of England where both found fame, and a little fortune. Yet both had to travel far away from home to achieve that celebrity - all the way to Lancashire and Yorkshire from a place called Tiger Bay. There was a time when that dock area of Cardiff achieved a rare mystical status in the eyes of young Rugby League fans, such was its fame for producing some of the game's most exotic stars. It was hard to believe that this place called Tiger Bay was not somewhere on a sunkissed Caribbean coastline but was, in reality, a rough and tough area around the Cardiff docks.

Tiger Bay was notorious for being a place where merchant seamen from all over the world would arrive and only stay for as long as it took to unload and reload their boats. Trade from the docks around Tiger Bay reached its pinnacle just before the First World War in 1913 when some 10.7 million tons of coal was exported from the port. After that war the boom in shipping in Cardiff continued with 122 shipping companies in existence in 1920 - but the years of the depression were to follow and after the Second World War coal exports began to decline, fnally ceasing in 1964.

Tiger Bay became famous for its very well integrated multi-racial community, as people from many different parts of the world came to call it home. Its best known celebrity resident may have been the singer Shirley Bassey, but when it came to sporting heroes - apart from heavyweight boxing champion Joe Erskine - it was Rugby

League which came to be synonymous with Tiger Bay with three players - Billy Boston, Johnny Freeman and Colin Dixon, plus another, Clive Sullivan, from nearby Splott - emerging to be recognised among its all-time greats.

Significantly, all of that famous quartet were black sportsmen which, some might suggest, tells us a lot about attitudes in Rugby Union at the time Boston, Freeman, Dixon and Sullivan were emerging - and of their hopes of ever winning a Welsh cap in their country's chosen code of rugby. Instead, they switched to Rugby League where they were welcomed with open arms in the north of England.

Billy Boston and Johnny Freeman were school mates in Tiger Bay. "It was a beautiful place to live," recalled Billy. "Everybody got on and there was every nationality under the sun in Tiger Bay. I lived at number seven Angelina Street and Joe Erskine lived at number eleven. Shirley Bassey and Johnny Freeman lived just around the corner."

The budding rugby players like Boston and Freeman first learned their skills in a team that came to be known as the "Kyaks" - the Cardiff International Athletic Club, which originally began as a club for the young sportsmen of Tiger Bay and which embraced a wide variety of racial backgrounds. Yet Tiger Bay's contribution to Rugby League had begun many years before Billy Boston came on the scene, because it had also been home to the one and only Gus Risman. The young Augustus John Risman had attended the same South Church Street School in Tiger Bay at which Boston and Freeman were later to becom pupils; and Risman's father kept a boarding house for seamen in this docklands area of Cardiff.

Writing in his autobiography *"Rugby Renegade"* published in 1958, Gus Risman had this to say about Tiger Bay: *"It is a wonderful area because for many years people of every nationality, colour, race and religion have lived, worked and played there without a hint of intolerance or bitterness. A spot of the Tiger Bay spirit might well have been the making of this game of rugby."*

(Above) **GUS RISMAN** as a young man in 1932, described Tiger Bay as a wonderful place. He headed north from Cardiff to become one of the greatest figures in the history of Rugby League. *(Right)* **COLIN DIXON** in action for the Welsh international team in the late 1970s - Colin had an exemplary career.

With both Gus Risman and Billy Boston included, two of the original nine members of Rugby League's "Hall of Fame" were boys from Tiger Bay. Yet, despite the fame of Billy and of Johnny Freeman, many old-timers in the area that once was Tiger Bay, will quickly quote the name of Colin Dixon when it comes to remembering the greatest sportsmen they have known.

Colin - who also was a pupil at South Church Sreet School like Risman and Boston - came north to Rugby League with Halifax at 17-years-of-age. In his 20-year career as a player he was to play a remarkable 738 first-class games, putting him sixth in the all-time list of most appearances in the history of the game, behind only Jim Sullivan, Gus Risman, Neil Fox, Jeff Grayshon and Graham Idle. Just think, no less than three of the game's top six appearance-makers in history hailed from Cardiff and two, specifically, from Tiger Bay.

The old terraces of Tiger Bay were demolished in the 1960s, and today - in the 21st Century - this former dock area has been rebranded as Cardiff Bay and totally transformed due to the building of the Cardiff Barrage. But for Rugby League fans of a certain age, mention of the name Tiger Bay will always bring a warm glow of recognition. Even for those folk from the north who had never heard of the Cairo Cafe or Sophia Street, Tiger Bay was a place of mystique and one which kept on unearthing such rare treasures for Rugby League.

MAINE ROAD

(Right) Workington's JOHNNY LAWRENSON is sent clear down the wing in Town's 1951 Final win over Warrington at Maine Road, Manchester.

Grounds fit for CHAMPIONS

RUGBY League's long established tradition of having a play-off Final to decide its end of season Champions was in rude good health in 2007, with another huge crowd at Old Trafford to see St.Helens play Leeds to decide the title winners plus a new record attendance set at Headingley for the National League Grand Finals won by Castleford and Featherstone.

Old Trafford, and now hopefully Headingley, have become the established showpiece venues for the modern game's Grand Finals but, in years gone by, two stadiums became synonymous with the Championship Final. One on the west of the Pennines at Maine Road, home of Manchester City Football Club, the other in Yorkshire at Odsal Stadium, home of Bradford Northern. They were the only two stadiums big enough in the Rugby League heartlands to accomodate the big crowds that Championship Finals attracted. With the Challenge Cup Final so successfully established at Wembley, the Championship Final which followed was seen as the north's own chance to stage its showpiece event.

In the years after the War, every Championship Final from 1946 through to 1962 was staged, first at Maine Road and then at Odsal - with the exception of the 1952 Final between Wigan and Bradford which was played at Huddersfield Town's Leeds Road ground. In those years the highest crowds at the respective venues was 75,194 at Maine Road in 1949 for Huddersfield v. Warrington, and 83,190 at Odsal in 1960 for Wigan v. Wakefield.

ODSAL STADIUM

(Left) Oldham winger JOHN ETTY has beaten Hull's hooker Tommy Harris and is about to score a try in the Roughyeds 1957 Championship Final win at Odsal Stadium. John and Oldham celebrated the 50th anninvesary of that title win in 2007.

Once of Warrington, Bradford and Rochdale, but he'll always be

JOHN WOODS - A LEIGH CHAMPION

LEIGH will always remember him as one of their favourite sons and greatest players - although John Woods also shone in the colours of Warrington, Bradford Northern and Rochdale Hornets. But when it came to sheer class, they've never seen better from a local boy at Hilton Park.

He was the idol of the Leigh crowd for nine seasons the pinnacle of which was captaining them to the Championship in 1982. In that time he played 302 first team games for Leigh, wracking up a massive total of 2,172 points which was just 22 short of Jimmy Ledgard's all-time Leigh club record. With effortless class, Woods would ghost through defences with a confidence that belied a fellow who was so quiet and modest off the field.

It was Geoff Fletcher, then the "A" team coach, who prompted Leigh to sign John Woods after he had graduated though their successful Colts team. John had played for Great Britain in the very first Colts international against France in Cannes in 1976 and in the senior ranks he rapidly won caps for Lancashire and then England. He went on to play in seven Tests for Great Britain (plus another four as a substitute) and was a Lions tourist in 1979.

As a stand-off and centre, John Woods was one of the few world stars of the British team during some of the tough times of the late 1970s and early '80s. He left Leigh in 1985 to sign for Bradford, but he'll always be a Leigh Champion.

for **BRADFORD NORTHERN**

for **WARRINGTON**

for **LEIGH**

for **GREAT BRITAIN**

JOHN WOODS graced the international stage for many years. *(Left)* He is pictured playing in the 1989 American Challenge Match in Milwaukee, Wisconsin. *(Right)* Playing for Great Britain in a Test match against France

THEY WERE ONE OF RUGBY LEAGUE'S MOST FAMILIAR LANDMARKS

The ODSAL STEPS

PHOTO by EDDIE WHITHAM

MANY Rugby League grounds have had their own particular landmarks which have endeared them to spectators over the years, some better known than others like, for example: the pavilion at Wigan's Central Park; the ramp down which players would walk to enter the field from the old dressing-room corner at Headingley; or the walk around the cricket pitch to the grandstand at Fartown.

All just distant memories now, but one never to be forgotten by anyone who experienced them will always be the Odsal steps. The long walk down from the dressing-rooms at Odsal top, into the cavernous bowl of Bradford which awaited them, was a journey taken by thousands of players as some of the game's most famous events were about to unfold. Those dressing-rooms were first opened in 1935, and for the ensuing 50 years the long descent to the pitch was part and parcel of matches at Odsal.

Bradford Northern players became used to it, some enjoyed the pre-match banter with spectators and their shouts of encouragement as they made their way down. But for visiting teams and, most especially for harassed referees, running the gauntlet of such masses, could be a very daunting experience - more often on the long climb back after the match was over if things hadn't gone the way of the home side.

For referees of a more nervous disposition, the long walk back to the safety of the dressing-rooms could be a scary experience, and they would be anxious to see a police-officer clearing a safe path ahead. Not so for the doyen of referees, the "Sergeant Major" Eric Clay, who more than once found himself incurring the wrath of some sections of the crowd, but never felt threatened by them. Mr.Clay said his greater concern going up the Odsal steps was about flatulent police horses leading the way.

"The spectators didn't bother me, but I was always worried about walking too close behind some of those horses," Eric always used to joke.

On the day Bradford Northern recorded their lowest ever crowd when just 324 spectators attended a match versus Barrow on 23rd November, 1963, it is quite likely the players were able to have a chat with all of them as they made their way up and down the Odsal steps. But, in marked contrasts, the stadium also housed some of the biggest crowds the Rugby League game has ever known during the years when the players would have to push their way through huge masses of humanity to get to and from the pitch.

That was never more true, of course, than on that famous Wednesday evening of May 5th, 1954, when a world record attendance of 102,569 (and estimated by most wise judges as actually over 120,000) packed into the Odsal bowl for the replayed Challenge Cup Final between Halifax and Warrington.

(Above) Neil Fox leads the Bradford Northern team down the Odsal steps.
(Left) Warrington and Halifax emerge from the steps and through the world record crowd, estimated at 120,000, on that famous night in May, 1954 at Odsal stadium.

How the nerves of those players must have been jangling that night as they made the torturous descent down those wooden sleepers under the gaze of such a huge crowd. It was a pre-match ritual that could turn even the most experienced players' legs to jelly.

John McKeown, the old Whitehaven full-back, always recalled that nervous walk down the Odsal steps when talking about his team's infamous Cup semi-final defeat to Leeds in 1957. *"We'd never seen a crowd as big as that before (just a few short of 50,000 was the official figure) and when some of the lads saw all those thousands of people, and then we had to make that slow walk down the steps knowing that all those eyes were watching us, the nerves got to them. If we could have just run out onto the pitch and kicked off, they would have been fine - but when you had to stop and look at that huge bowl full of people, it got the butterflies going."*

All that changed at Odsal in 1985, when new dressing rooms were built at pitch level and the steps were no more. One of Rugby League's most famous rituals had passed into memory.

Some of Rugby League's favourite double-acts
CLASSIC HALF-BACK PARTNERSHIPS

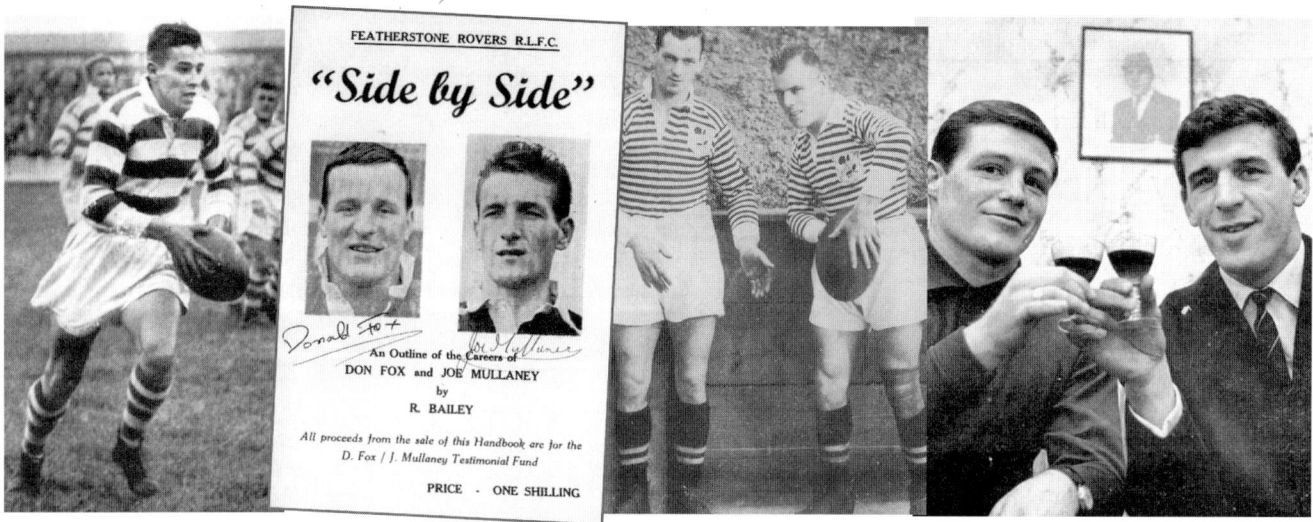

Memories of some of famous half-back partnerships. From left to right: STAN KIELTY, one half of the inseparable Halifax pairing of Dean and Kielty; DON FOX and JOE MULLANEY celebrating their benefit "side by side" with Featherstone Rovers; the two Tommies, SHANNON and McCUE of Widnes pictured together in their Lancashire county outfits; KEITH HEPWORTH and ALAN HARDISTY - "Heppy and Chuck" - pictured as they made a toast to celebrate their testimonial with Castleford.

LIKE strawberries and cream or fish and chips, some things were meant to go together. In the entertainment world, you could not mention Laurel without Hardy, Morecambe without Wise, Torvill without Dean, or even Sooty without Sweep!

And in Rugby League, some names will always be linked together automatically as members of an irresistable partnership rather than as two individuals.

They come from the time when Rugby League was still a game of specialised positions, when the thought of a scrum-half playing hooker or a stand-off playing prop would have been absolutely laughable - but believe us, we saw it happen during the 2007 season!

A good half-back partnership was always a key to having a successful team, and the best partnerships were the ones which stayed together for years enabling each partner to get to know the other's play inside out. All the game's great half-back partners would say there was a certain telepathy between them and their sidekick, to the point that each didn't have to think about what the other was going to do - they just knew in advance.

Every Rugby League supporter in years gone by would know the names of the classic half-back partnerships, the most famous being: **Hardisty and Hepworth** of Castleford; **Dean and Kielty** of Halifax; **Shannon and McCue** of Widnes; **Shoebottom and Seabourne** of Leeds; and **Fox and Mullaney** of Featherstone Rovers. Longevity was a part of their success and the instant recognition their names generated when spoken of in the same breath, indeed some would take 10-year benefits together.

Some moved lock, stock and barrell in a double-deal to another club as they were regarded as so inseparable, as when both Alan Hardisty and Keith Hepworth left hometown Castleford to sign for Leeds. Meanwhile, Ken Dean and Stan Kielty of Halifax were sometimes portrayed by newspaper cartoonists of their day as Siamese twins, so closely were they linked.

Anticipation of famous half-back duos

The anticipation of seeing the famous half-back partnerships in action together used be one of the great thrills of Rugby League; how about these names to provoke a few memories: Archer and Roper of Workington Town; Poynton and Holliday of Wakefield Triniy; Horne and Toohey of Barrow; Mountford and Bradshaw of Wigan; Willie Davies and Donald Ward of Bradford Northern; Ray Price and Gerry Helme of Warrington; Cliff Hill and Frankie Parr of Wigan. The history books tell us of the exploits of great pre-War half-back duos like Emlyn Jenkins and Billy Watkins of the famous Salford "Red Devils" of the 1930s, who also played at international level together; and at nearby Swinton there was another international duo in Billo Rees and Bryn Evans.

In more modern times, who could forget the creative hub of the Edwards and Gregory partnership in the all-conquering Wigan teams of the late 1980s and early '90s, whilst in Australia the brilliant Kenny and Sterling duo had much to do not only with the successes of Jack Gibson's Parramatta teams but also the 1982 "Invincible" Kangaroos. Subsequently, the Aussies saw the value of a great half-back partnership with Lewis and Langer at State level and then Newcastle's Johns brothers in club football. Whilst for the French international team, the six and seven duo of Dumas and Entat was as stable and important as any they have known.

DANNY McGUIRE & ROB BURROW

MODERN DAY STARS AT LEEDS

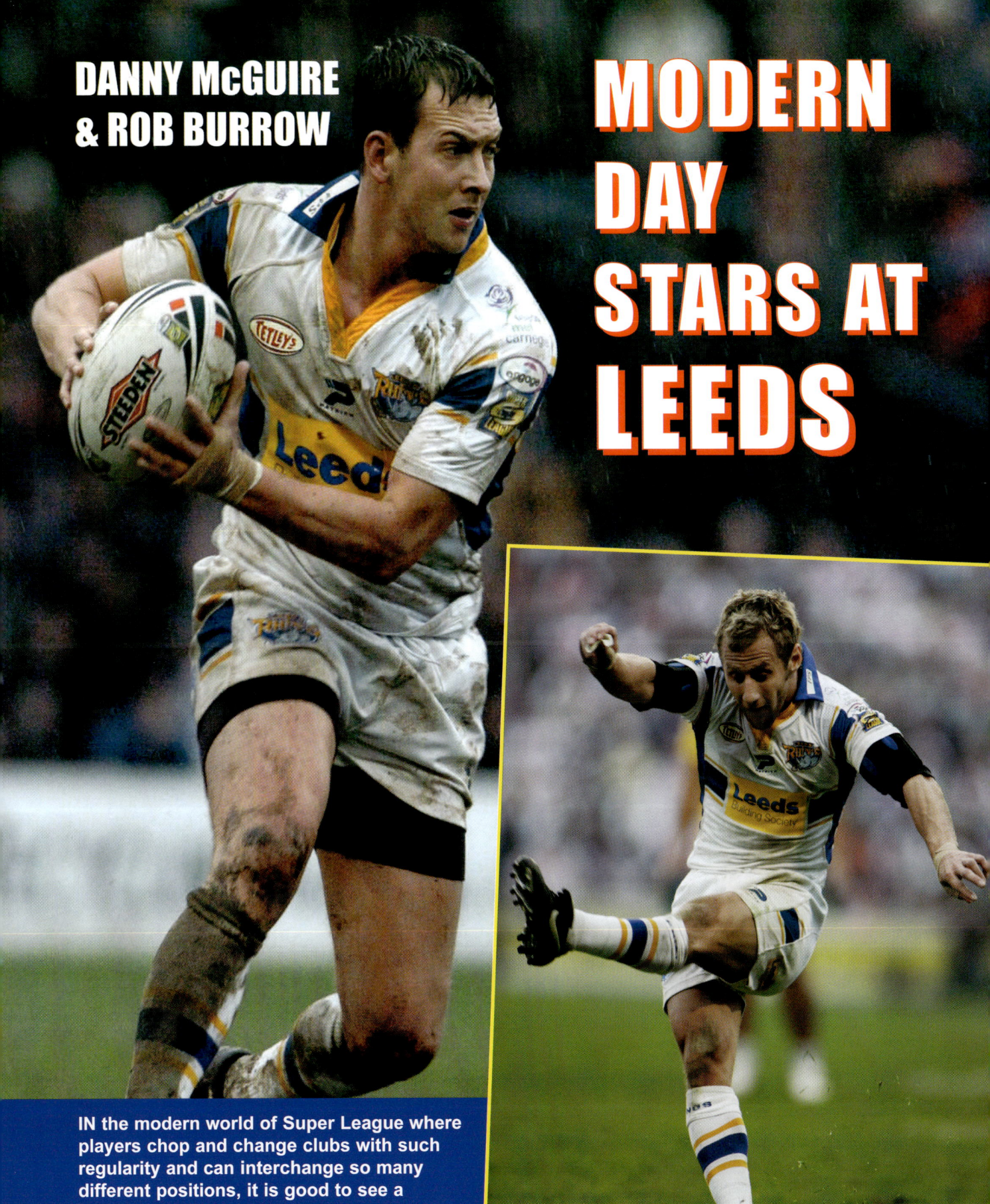

IN the modern world of Super League where players chop and change clubs with such regularity and can interchange so many different positions, it is good to see a long-term half-back partnership endure like that of DANNY McGUIRE and ROB BURROW at Leeds. They also played together as the Great Britain half-backs in 2007, and continue to follow in the much revered footsteps of Shoebottom and Seabourne at Headingley.

Photos by
ANDREW VARLEY
Picture Agency

WARRINGTON'S other BEVAN

A try by John Bevan at Widerspool versus Bradford Northern.

Photos by EDDIE WHITHAM

THE name *Bevan* is the most famous of any established in the history of the Warrington Rugby League club and every supporter knows all about the legendary feats of the game's greatest try-scorer, Brian Bevan. But, for another generation of Wire fans from the mid-1970s to the mid-'80s, it was another wingman called Bevan who stole their hearts and became their swashbuckling hero on the flanks at Wilderspool.

John Bevan, whose style as a block-busting powerhouse of a winger could not have been more different to that of his famous namesake Brian, was one of the most popular and successful converts from Welsh Rugby Union after he came north to Warrington in 1973. John had been a big star in the fabled British Lions touring team of 1971 which beat the All Blacks in New Zealand, and he took to the League game like a natural, becoming a dual-code Lion when he toured with the Great Britain team in 1974. In all, John Bevan scored 201 tries for Warrington in his 12-year career in the primrose and blue - many of them were matchwinners produced with the flambouyant style and power which ensures they'll never forget the *other* Bevan.

OH for the VIDEO REF!

HOW THE HISTORY OF CUMBRIAN RUGBY LEAGUE COULD HAVE BEEN SO DIFFERENT

The Video Referee in today's game may be infuriating when over-used - but how things could have been different in the game's history if such technology had always been around. The Cumbrian clubs, Whitehaven and Workington, had vastly different kinds of luck in their Challenge Cup semi-finals of 1957 and 1952 respectively - and one got Wembley and the other didn't...

(TOP PICTURE): Odsal 1957 - as Leeds winger George Broughton squeezes in for one of his two tries against Whitehaven, he has clearly already hit the corner-flag before the ball has been grounded. Yet a try was given and Leeds eventually won by one point, 10-9, to go to Wembley. *(LOWER PICTURE):* Central Park 1952 - Barrow prop John Pearson clearly has the ball down on the line, but referee Laurie Thorpe is unsighted and by the time he got there, Workington defenders had turned Pearson onto his back, so the try was disallowed. Barrow lost 5-2 and it was Workington who went on to lift the Cup at Wembley.

33

WHEN 22,000 CROWD WATCHED

BLACKPOOL has a team in the professional ranks of the Rugby League as the year 2008 approached, maintaining a dream that was born way back in 1954 with the birth of the original Blackpool Borough.

In 2007, the Blackpool players still wore the traditional colours of tangerine, black and white - alebit in a format unrecognisable from the design which was so unique and popular in the days of the old Borough club - and, in another time honoured Blackpool tradition, they spent much of their season with a Wiganer at the helm after Andy Gregory came in to coach them.

But, sadly, the Blackpool team of 2007 (nicknamed not the Borough, but the Panthers) did not win a single match throughout their whole campaign in National League Two, finishing 15 points behind the second bottom side Gateshead. And the current Blackpool team for their home ground play as the guests of the Fylde Rugby Union club.

Like several other clubs in the lower tier of the National League, Blackpool could only number their crowds in the low hundreds, which makes it dreadfully difficult to be able to maintain a semi-professional club. All this was a far cry from those days of such optimism in the mid-1950s when the Blackpool Borough club was launched after several years of excited speculation about the merits of establishing a Rugby League team in what was then regarded as the entertainment capital of the north of England.

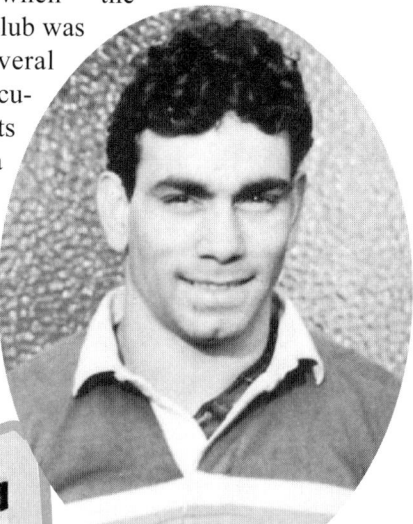

WALLY McARTHUR *(above)* the flying Australian winger who played for Blackpool Borough in their 1957 Cup-tie against Leigh at Bloomfield Road.

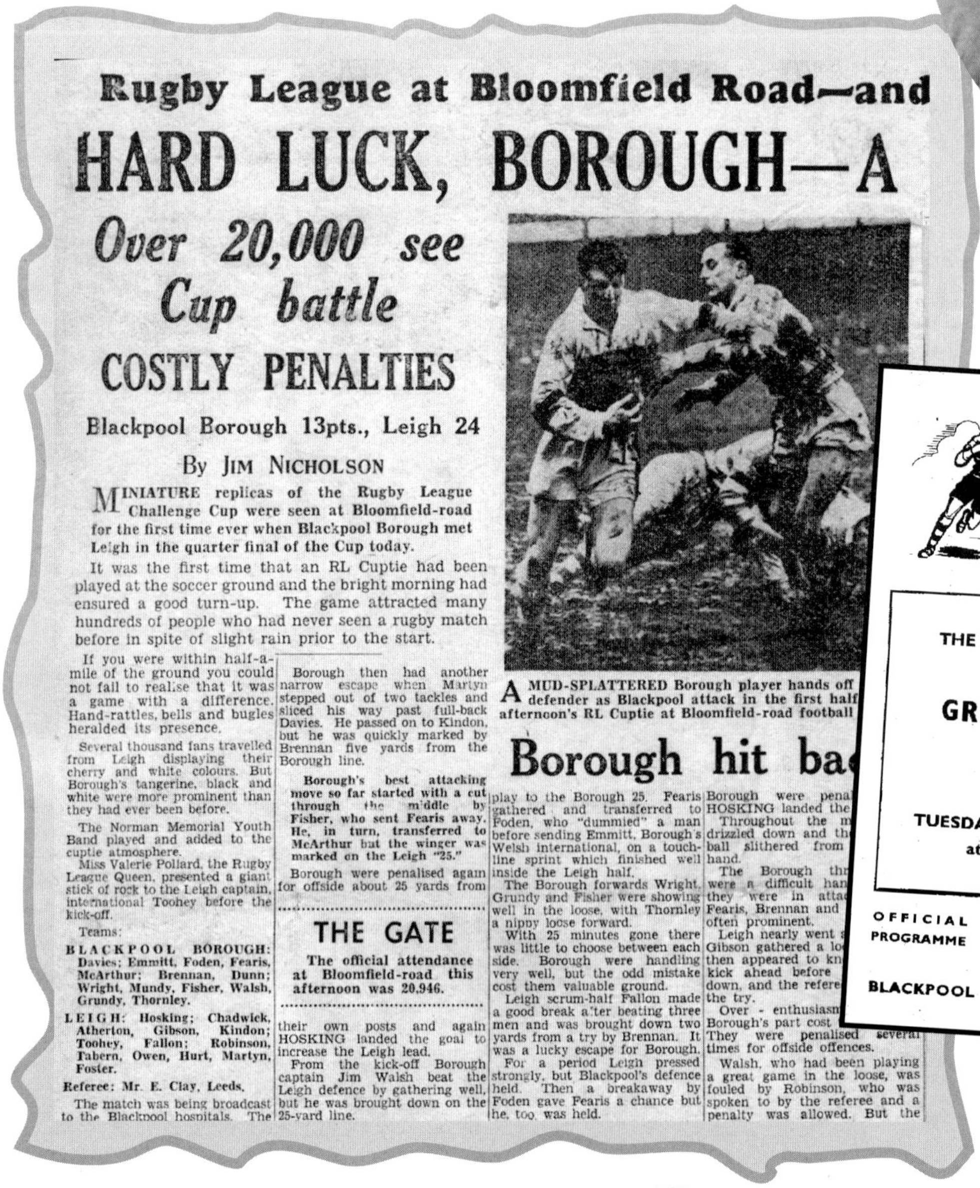

Rugby League at Bloomfield Road—and

HARD LUCK, BOROUGH—A

Over 20,000 see Cup battle

COSTLY PENALTIES

Blackpool Borough 13pts., Leigh 24

By JIM NICHOLSON

MINIATURE replicas of the Rugby League Challenge Cup were seen at Bloomfield-road for the first time ever when Blackpool Borough met Leigh in the quarter final of the Cup today.

It was the first time that an RL Cuptie had been played at the soccer ground and the bright morning had ensured a good turn-up. The game attracted many hundreds of people who had never seen a rugby match before in spite of slight rain prior to the start.

If you were within half-a-mile of the ground you could not fail to realise that it was a game with a difference. Hand-rattles, bells and bugles heralded its presence.

Several thousand fans travelled from Leigh displaying their cherry and white colours. But Borough's tangerine, black and white were more prominent than they had ever been before.

The Norman Memorial Youth Band played and added to the cuptie atmosphere.

Miss Valerie Pollard, the Rugby League Queen, presented a giant stick of rock to the Leigh captain, international Toohey before the kick-off.

Teams:

BLACKPOOL BOROUGH: Davies; Emmitt, Foden, Fearis, McArthur; Brennan, Dunn; Wright, Mundy, Fisher, Walsh, Grundy, Thornley.

LEIGH: Hosking; Chadwick, Atherton, Gibson, Kindon; Toohey, Fallon; Robinson, Tabern, Owen, Hurt, Martyn, Foster.

Referee: Mr. E. Clay, Leeds.

The match was being broadcast to the Blackpool hospitals. The

Borough then had another narrow escape when Martyn stepped out of two tackles and sliced his way past full-back Davies. He passed on to Kindon, but he was quickly marked by Brennan five yards from the Borough line.

Borough's best attacking move so far started with a cut through the middle by Fisher, who sent Fearis away. He, in turn, transferred to McArthur but the winger was marked on the Leigh "25."

Borough were penalised again for offside about 25 yards from

THE GATE

The official attendance at Bloomfield-road this afternoon was 20,946.

their own posts and again HOSKING landed the goal to increase the Leigh lead.

From the kick-off Borough captain Jim Walsh beat the Leigh defence by gathering well, but he was brought down on the 25-yard line.

A MUD-SPLATTERED Borough player hands off defender as Blackpool attack in the first half afternoon's RL Cuptie at Bloomfield-road football

Borough hit ba

play to the Borough 25. Fearis gathered and transferred to Foden, who "dummied" a man before sending Emmitt, Borough's Welsh international, on a touch-line sprint which finished well inside the Leigh half.

The Borough forwards Wright, Grundy and Fisher were showing well in the loose, with Thornley a nippy loose forward.

With 25 minutes gone there was little to choose between each side. Borough were handling very well, but the odd mistake cost them valuable ground.

Leigh scrum-half Fallon made a good break a'ter beating three men and was brought down two yards from a try by Brennan. It was a lucky escape for Borough.

For a period Leigh pressed strongly, but Blackpool's defence held. Then a breakaway by Foden gave Fearis a chance but he, too, was held.

Borough were pena HOSKING landed the

Throughout the m drizzled down and th ball slithered from hand.

The Borough thr were a difficult han they were in attac Fearis, Brennan and often prominent.

Leigh nearly went Gibson gathered a lo then appeared to kn kick ahead before down, and the refere the try.

Over - enthusiasm Borough's part cost They were penalised several times for offside offences.

Walsh, who had been playing a great game in the loose, was fouled by Robinson, who was spoken to by the referee and a penalty was allowed. But the

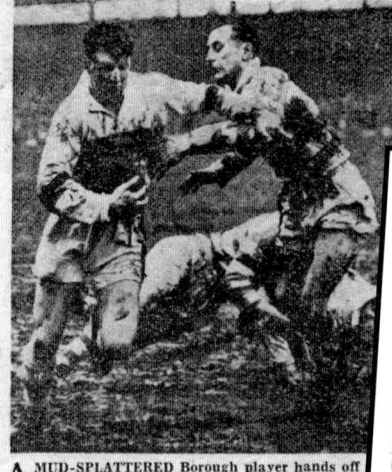

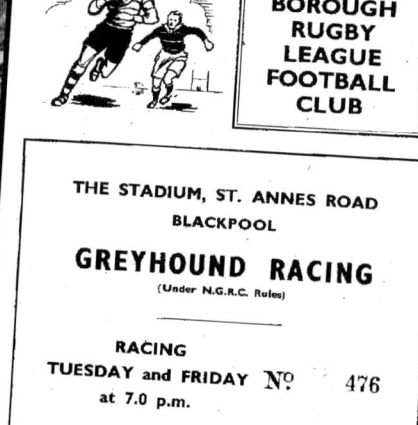

(Above) Official programme for the Blackpool v Leigh game at Bloomfield Road in March 1957.

RUGBY LEAGUE AT BLACKPOOL

Never was that excitement seen at more fever pitch in Blackpool than in March 1957, when Borough drew Leigh at home in the Challenge Cup third round. After excellent away wins at Rochdale and Wakefield in the first two rounds, Blackpool found themselves in a Cup quarter-final in just their third season in the game. *"Just two steps away from the glittering prize of an appearance at Wembley,"* was how it was described in the Borough programme for the match against Leigh.

Such was the magical appeal of the Challenge Cup in those days, as soon as the draw gave Blackpool a home tie, they knew their small ground at the St.Annes Road Stadium would not be able to cope with the demand for places. So, the Borough directors turned to their soccer neighbours and were immdiately given an invitation to stage the match at their Bloomfield Road football ground. Remember, at the time, Blackpool were one of the great powers at the top level of English football and, just four years earlier, had won the most famous of all F.A. Cup Finals when Stanley Matthews weaved his magic at Wembley.

The directors of the Borough Rugby League club said they were *"greatly touched, and indeed overwhelmed, by the generous gesture of the Blackpool Football Club"* and in a statement in their programme they commented: *"Let it be known that, when approached for the use of the ground, there was no haggling over a rental fee. The (Football Club) Board were anxious to help our pogress in the Cup competition in every possible way, and we are privileged to stage the game today at a purely nominal, almost 'give away' rental."*

It was not the first time Rugby League had been played at Bloomfield Road, in the autumn of 1955, at the start of the Borough's econd season, they had drawn a crowd of over 12,000 for their match against the New Zealand touring team. But nothing could compare with the Blackpool record-breaking attendance of over 22,000 which turned out for the Cup-tie with Leigh on 9th March, 1957. The official figure of paying spectators was given as 20,946. After an exciting battle in muddy conditions, Blackpool's Cup dream came to end as Leigh won 24-13 - penalty goals by Leigh full-back Joe Hosking edging them ahead and keeping them just in front of a brave and determined Borough team, who scored tries by Gilly Wright, Terry Dunn and Jim Grundy plus two goals by full-back Stan Davies. But the abiding memory was to be that record crowd, the day 22,000 people packed in to watch Blackpool Borough play a home match in the shadow of the famous Blackpool tower. Bloomfield Road still stages Rugby League as the venue of the Northern Rail Cup Final.

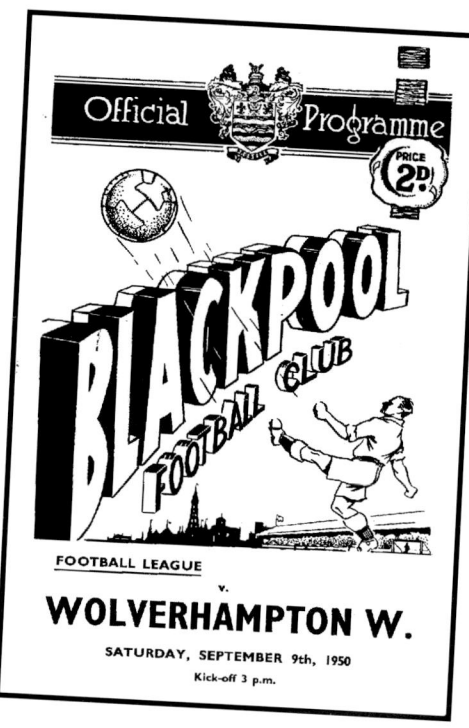

(Above) **This was the type of programme the good folk of Blackpool were more used to seeing at Bloomfield Road in the 1950s - this one in the Football League versus Wolves**

This was how one Sunday newspaper pictured Blackpool Borough's opening try in that 1957 cup tie against Leigh at Bloomfield Road. The top picture shows Blackpool prop Gilly Wright breaking through the Leigh defence; he then took a return pass from scrum-half Terry Dunn to tear over to score, closely watched by referee Clay.

Early days of advertising by Rugby League star players

ENDORSED BY BRITAIN'S BEST

THE world's top sports stars in the 21st Century make a fortune in having their name attached to the endorsement of various products and services - and the term "image rights" is a crucial part of many lucrative contract discussions.

Alas for Rugby League players, certainly in Europe, the game's lack of appreciation means they are not part of this world of multi-million dollar deals. Paul Sculthorpe as the face of Gillette's Rugby League sponsorship campaign in recent years was probably the best our men could get!

However, long before the late Mark McCormack started building the new industry of sports sponsorships, and even longer before anybody had heard of Tiger Woods or *Nike*, British Rugby League stars were, in their own little way, being asked to use their fame and celebrity to endorse products.

A flick back through old copies of the *"Rugby League Gazette"* or programmes from the mid-1950s revealed the four advertisements illustrated on this page. The esteem held for Great Britain Rugby League captains meant they were very respected and widely recognised figures, as we can see with: **Jim Brough** advertising the omnipresent Jim Windsor's pools; **Dave Valentine** - fresh from his triumph in the first World Cup - telling us he knew the value of a good watch; and 1957 World Cup captain **Alan Prescott** saying how proud his team were to wear *"Holeproof Zealon"* socks, something his predecessor on the 1954 Lions tour, **Dickie Williams**, along with colleagues Brian Briggs and Jack Wilkinson, was also happy to endorse.

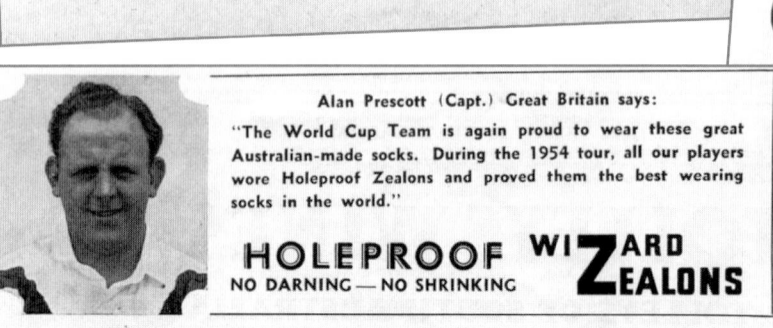

CLUB NOSTALGIA

The following section of this Annual presents our nostalgia pages on all your favourite clubs of old in the Rugby League

(Pictured) A Saturday afternoon in the 1960s at Wilderspool as Warrington's Brian Glover and Bill Payne ensure this Wakefield Trinity attacker goes over the touch-line, and the touch-judge agrees. (Photo by Eddie Whitham).

BARROW

CLUB FORMED IN 1875 - JOINED NORTHERN UNION 1900

Club Nostalgia

10 HISTORIC MILESTONES

1900 - 1st September - first game in Northern Union, Barrow lose at Runcorn 10-5.

1931 - Craven Park opened, first game on 29th August sees visitors Swinton win - crowd 16,167.

1938 - Barrow reach first Challenge Cup Final, but lose in last minute at Wembley 7-4 to Salford.

1938 - Record attendance at Craven Park as 21,651 watch Barrow v. Salford league match.

1943 - Barrow's greatest hero, Willie Horne, makes his debut and by the time he retires in 1959 has become the town's most famous icon.

1951 - Second Wembley Final for Barrow, but the Cup goes to Wigan after 10-nil defeat.

1955 - Barrow's greatest moment as they win the Challenge Cup, captained by Willie Horne, beating Workington at Wembley 21-12. Second-rower Jack Grundy wins the Lance Todd trophy.

1957 - Third Wembley Final in six years but Barrow lose 9-7 to Leeds. Winger Jimmy Lewthwaite scores a club record 50 tries in the season and then retires after a wonderful career.

MIKE MURRAY - at Wembley for Barrow in 1967.

1967 - Barrow's fifth and last Cup Final led by Jim Challinor against Featherstone Rovers.

1983 - Barrow win Lancashire Cup, captained by prop Alan Hodkinson they beat Widnes in the Final 12-8, David Cairns the man-of-the-match.

(Above) PHIL ATKINSON - an outstanding servant to the Barrow club for 15 years, hung up his boots at the end of an excellent 2007 campaign. Ulverston lad Phil made a huge contribution to keeping the flag flying for Barrow Rugby at Craven Park.

This Barrow team group is from the mid-1960s pictured at Craven Park. Left to right, *(Standing)*: Keith Irving, Eddie Tees, Bill Burgess, Ivor Kelland, Mick Ducie, Maurice Redhead, Tommy Smales. *(In front)*: Bob Wear, David Black, Bob Little, Jim Challinor (Captain-coach), Les Woolveridge and Billy Skeels. Within a couple of years, Challinor had moulded a side which won through to the Challenge Cup Final in 1967, but only Tees, Burgess, Kelland and Redhead from this team pictured joined their player-coach at Wembley where, as fate would have it, Tommy Smales was to star for their opponents, Featherstone.

DO YOU KNOW?
Who was the last Barrow player to play for Great Britain down-under against Australia and New Zealand?

BATLEY
CLUB FORMED IN 1880 - NORTHERN UNION FOUNDER MEMBER 1895

Club Nostalgia

Batley team pictured at Mount Pleasant in the 1971-72 season. Left to right, (Standing): Mr. Leslie Driver (Chairman), D.Secker, J.Bell, J.Thomas, S.Greenhoff, C.Tyson, P.Doyle, D.Brooker, E.Hepworth, John Westbury (Coach). (In front): T.Oldroyd, U.Piwinski, G.Butterfield, P.Holmes (Captain), I.Watts, G.Marsh and A.Edwards. Mascot: M.Wilson.

10 HISTORIC MILESTONES

1895 - 7th September - Batley play first game in Northern Union, beat Hull 7-3 at Mount Pleasant.

1897 - Batley become very first winners of the Challenge Cup, defeating St.Helens 10-3 in the inaugural final at Headingley.

1898 - Batley retain the Challenge Cup beating Bradford 7-nil in the final.

1901 - The Gallant Youths win their third Challenge Cup in five years, led by Joe Oakland this time they triumph over Warrington in the final.

1912 - Batley win the Yorkshire Cup for the first and only time, beating Hull in the final at Leeds.

1924 - Their greatest achievement - Batley are crowned Rugby League Champions, captained by Ike Fowler they beat Wigan in the Final.

1925 - Record attendance set at Mount Pleasant as 23,989 watch cup-tie against Leeds.

1980 - Batley celebrate their centenary season, and beat Fulham in designated centenary match.

1990 - Batley's favourite son and former wing star, John Etty, opens the new Heritage Stand.

1998 - Now known as the Bulldogs, Batley win the short-lived Trans-Pennine Cup for the lower divisions, beating Oldham in the final at Mount Pleasant - this after being denied promotion to the top division in 1995 due to the new Super League.

(Below) JOHN FOX in action for Batley in a match against York at Mount Pleasant. Prop-forward Fox was a great servant to the Gallant Youths throughout the 1970s and his son, Deryck, was an international scrum-half.

DO YOU KNOW?
Who was the Batley player in the Great Britain team at Wembley in a 1963 Ashes Test match v Australia?

BLACKPOOL
CLUB FORMED IN 1954 - JOINED NORTHERN RUGBY LEAGUE 1954

Club Nostalgia

Memories of the tangerine. black and white days at Borough Park - this Blackpool Borough team was pictured in April, 1966 before a match verus Barrow. They are, left to right: *(Standing):* **Farrell, Hill, Meakin, Belshaw, Winstanley, Seddon, Bowden, Abbey, Ainscough, Bob Rippon (kit-man).** *(Seated):* **Ince, Sullivan, Martin Dickens (Captain), Gee, Fairhurst and Holmes.**

10 HISTORIC MILESTONES

1954 - 14th August - first game in the Northern Rugby League, Blackpool Borough, player-coached by Ron Ryder, lose 40-3 away at Salford.

1955 - Borough play the New Zealand tourists and draw 24-24 in front of a 12,000 crowd.

1957 - Blackpool's record attendance set as 20,946 watch Challenge Cup-tie against Leigh played at the Bloomfield Road football ground.

1959 - The player who was to become the club's most famous product, Tommy Bishop, is signed from junior Rugby League.

1963 - 31st August - the club's new home ground, Borough Park, is opened as Blackpool beat Salford 36-16 in front of a crowd of over 5,000. Brian Bevan makes his debut.

1964 - Blackpool entertain Castleford in Cup quarter-final and, despite live t.v., set record attendance for Borough Park of 7,614.

1977 - Blackpool win through to their first major Final, the Players No.6 Trophy. Coached by Jim Crellin, they lose to Castleford in the Final.

1979 - Albert Fearnley revitalises the Borough and they win promotion to the First Division.

1987 - The end comes for Blackpool Borough as ground safety problem force them to quit Borough Park - and the club is moved to Springfield, Wigan.

2005 - A professional club returns to the seaside with the formation of Blackpool Panthers.

(Above) Blackpool winger **BRIAN OLSEN** in action against Rochdale Hornets at Borough Park in the 1967-68 season.
(Right) The popular Borough Supporters' Club Handbook.

DO YOU KNOW?
Who was the Blackpool Borough hooker who shared man-of-the-match in the 1977 Players No.6 Final?

BLACKPOOL BOROUGH Official Handbook 1966-67
RUGBY LEAGUE SUPPORTERS' CLUB

BRADFORD
CLUB FORMED IN 1863 - NORTHERN UNION FOUNDER MEMBER 1895

Club Nostalgia

10 HISTORIC MILESTONES

1895 - 7th September - first game in Northern Union, Bradford beat Wakefield Trinity 11-nil.

1904 - Bradford win their first Championship.

1907 - The title "Northern" is adopted after the old Bradford club turns to Association Football.

1934 - Odsal Stadium is opened and goes on to play a huge role in the history of the game, notably housing a world record crowd in 1954.

1947 - Bradford Northern, captained by the great Ernest Ward, take part in the first of three consecutive Wembley Challenge Cup finals.

1964 - Following the closure of the club in December 1963, a new Bradford Northern is born, largely inspired by two former players, Joe Phillips and Trevor Foster. Crowds flock back to Odsal and by 1965 Tommy Smales arrives to become Bradford's inspiration and new hero.

1980 - Under Peter Fox as coach, Northern win the first of two consecutive titles as the Champions of Rugby League.

1995 - A new image arrives as the old Northern tag is dropped and Bradford become the Bulls - with a new decade of success about to unfold.

1997 - With Robbie Paul as captain, Bradford with the Super League Championship title, after losing two Wembley Cup finals in 1996 and 1997.

2000 - Bradford win the Challenge Cup for the first time in 51 years, when they beat Leeds in a final played at Murrayfield in Edinburgh.

This Bradford Northern team group is from the late 1960s. Left to right, *(Standing):* Bob Taylor, Terry Price, Terry Ramshaw, Terry Clawson, David Hill, Mike Kelly, Ken Roberts, Johnny Rae. *(Seated):* Tony Fisher, Alan Rhodes, Alan Hepworth, Berwyn Jones, Alan Kellett, Bakary Diabira, Geoff Wriglesworth, Dave Stockwell and George Ambrum.

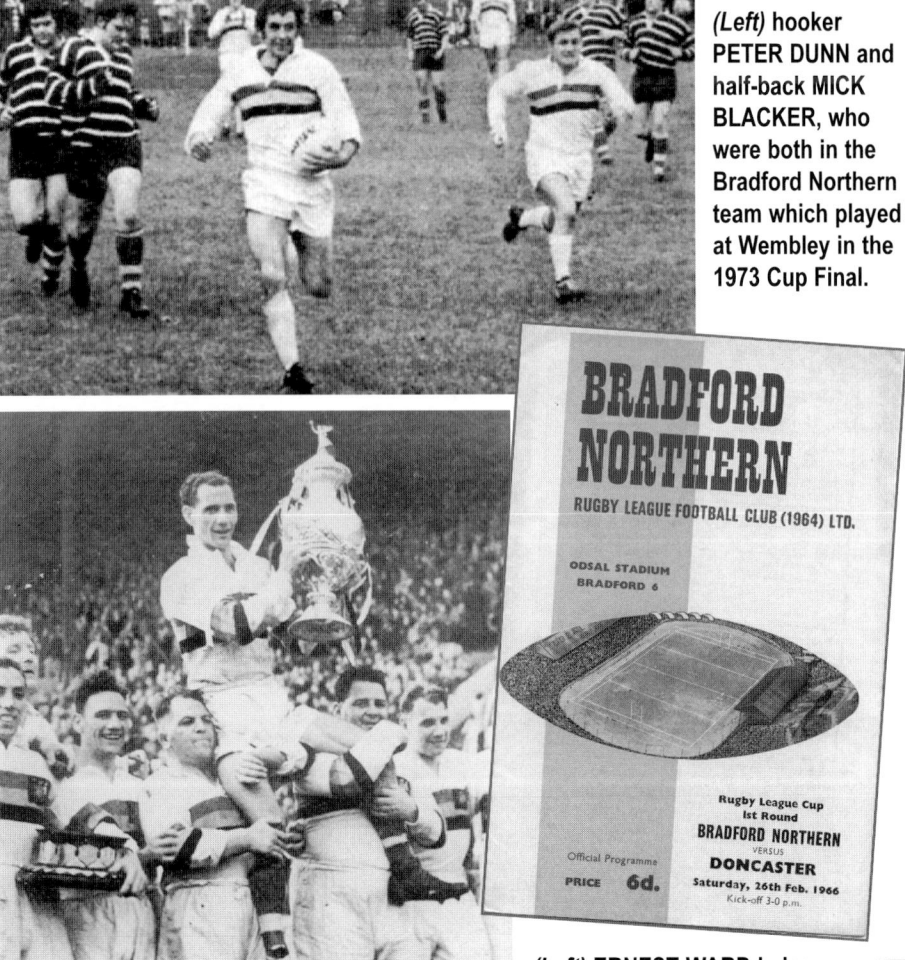

(Left) hooker PETER DUNN and half-back MICK BLACKER, who were both in the Bradford Northern team which played at Wembley in the 1973 Cup Final.

(Left) ERNEST WARD being chaired by happy Bradford team-mates after beating Halifax to win the Challenge Cup at Wembley in 1949.

DO YOU KNOW?
Which Bradford legend played his last match for the club in 1993 after a career of almost 600 games

41

BRAMLEY
CLUB FORMED IN 1880 - JOINED NORTHERN UNION 1896

Club Nostalgia

(Left) The Bramley team in the 1975-76 season, lining up at McClaren Field. This was when they were coached by Arthur Keegan with Maurice Bamford as his assistant. Left to right: *(Standing):* Alf Weston, Jack Austin, Dave Holdsworth, Tony Cheshire, Terry Dewhirst, Daniel Rowe, Ian Johnston, Ian Reed. *(In front):* Joe Johnson, John Hay, Keith Bollon, Barry Langton, Steve Bond, Parker and Billy Rowett.

10 HISTORIC MILESTONES

1896 - 5th September - first game in Northern Union, Bramley draw nil-nil at Heckmondwike.

1907 - Bramley host the very first tour match when Baskerville's famous All Golds from New Zealand beat them 25-6 at the Barley Mow.

1935 - Bramley are one of the pioneering clubs who travel to France to help promote the new game - they lose narrowly 25-19 to the inaugral French Cup winners Lyon-Villeurbanne.

1947 - The Barley Mow gets its record crowd as 12,600 attend a Bramley versus Leeds fixture.

1962 - The Villagers win a place in the new First Division and receive gold medals specially struck by their celebrity supporter, big Jim Windsor.

1966 - The Barley Mow is turned into McLaren Field and Bramley have a new home ground.

1973 - Bramley's finest hour as they cause an upset and win their first major trophy - beating Widnes 15-7 to take the BBC2 Floodlit Trophy, they are led by player-coach Arthur Keegan.

1977 - Wily Foxes guide Bramley to promotion to the elite division, Neil as captain and brother Peter the coach.

1995 - The Villagers lose their home at McLaren Field and play first at Clarence Field in Kirkstall before moving to Headingley in 1997.

1999 - Bramley's saddest day as the club folds up and no longer competes in the Rugby League. Some years later a new Bramley emerges as a community club playing out of Stanningley ARLFC.

(Above) DAVE SAMPSON on the the attack for Bramley against Widnes in the 1973 Floodlit Trophy Final - won by the Villagers.

(Above) In the Bramley boilerhouse - the Villagers' front-row in the 1980s: CHRIS BOWMAN, JEFF TENNANT and SAM WINDMILL.

DO YOU KNOW?
Who was the New Zealand Maori full-back who set new goals and points scoring records for Bramley?

CASTLEFORD
CLUB FORMED IN 1912 - JOINED NORTHERN RUGBY LEAGUE 1926

Club Nostalgia

(Above) Castleford and the joy of winning at Wembley in 1969. Captain Alan Hardisty and coach Derek Turner hold the Cup aloft as they are chaired by their happy team after beating Salford.

10 HISTORIC MILESTONES

1926 - 28th August - first game in the Northern Rugby League as Cas' lose 22-nil away at Hull.

1935 - Record attendance set at Wheldon Road as 25,449 crowd watch cup-tie with Hunslet.

1935 - Castleford win the Challenge Cup at Wembley for the first time, captained by Arthur Atkinson they beat Huddersfield 11-8 in the Final.

1939 - Castleford reach their first Championship Final, losing to Salford in front of a then record British crowd of 69,504 at Maine Road.

1958 - The half-back partnership which became synonymous with Castleford - Alan Hardisty and Keith Hepworth - make their first team debuts.

1965 - "Classy Cas" of the sixties are in full swing as they become the very first winners of the BBC2 Floodlit Trophy. Led by Hardisty they go on to with the compeititon for three successive years.

1969 - Castleford win the Challenge Cup beating Salford in the Final as Malcolm Reilly wins the Lance Todd trophy.

1970 - Back at Wembley Cas' retain the Challenge Cup as they beat Wigan. Bill Kirkbride wins the Lance Todd trophy.

1977 - Captained by Malcolm Reilly, Cas' win the Yorkshire Cup for the first time in their history.

1986 - Wembley glory as John Joyner skippers Castleford to the Challenge Cup, beating Hull K.R. 15-14. Bob Beardmore wins Lance Todd trophy.

JOHN JOYNER in action for Castleford against Ellery Hanley and Alan Redfearn of Bradford Northern in the early 1980s. Joyner captained Cas' to victory at Wembley in 1986 and served the club well.

DO YOU KNOW?
Who set a new tries in-a-season record for Castleford in 1963-64, and which player broke it 30 years later?

43

DEWSBURY
CLUB FORMED IN 1875 - JOINED NORTHERN UNION 1901

Club Nostalgia

Dewsbury at Crown Flatt in 1973, the team which became the Champions of the Rugby League. They are, left to right: (Standing): Brian Taylor, John Bates, Dick Lowe, Harry Beverley, Jeff Grayshon, Joe Whittington, Nigel Stephenson. (Seated): Terry Day, Steve Lee, Alan Agar, Mick Stephenson (captain), Greg Ashcroft, Alan Bates, John Clarke and Adrian Rushton.

10 HISTORIC MILESTONES

1901 - 7th September - first game in Northern Union, Dewsbury beat Sowerby Bridge 3-nil.

1912 - Dewsbury win the Challenge Cup, beating Oldham 8-5 in the Final at Headingley.

1920 - Record attendance set at Crown Flatt as 26,584 watch Yorkshire Cup tie against Halifax.

1925 - Dewsbury win the Yorkshire Cup for the first time and repeat the feat two years later.

1929 - Dewsbury play in the very first Wembley Cup Final, finishing runners-up to Wigan by 13-2.

1942-3 - With Eddie Waring as manager, Dewsbury dominate the game in war-time, winning the Challenge Cup, the Championship and the Yorkshire Cup - later their Championship win is declared void for fielding an ineligible player.

1947 - Skippered by Harry Royal, Dewsbury reach the Championship Final, losing to Wigan, but finish as Yorkshire League champions.

1973 - Their finest hour as Dewsbury are the Rugby League Champions - Mick Stephenson captaining them to glory over Leeds in the Final.

1991 - Crown Flatt stages its last game on 14th April, a 19-all draw with Barrow. Three years later Dewsbury open their new Owl Lane stadium.

2000 - Dewsbury win the Northern Ford Premiership, beating Leigh in the Grand Final, but do not get promotion to the Super League.

(Right) JIMMY LEDGARD - one of the finest players ever to wear the red, amber and black hoops of Dewsbury. One of Great Britain's World Cup winning heroes of 1954, Jimmy passed away in 2007.

DO YOU KNOW? Who was Dewsbury's coach when they won the Championship in 1973?

STEVO SCORES - Mick Stephenson dives over for a try for Dewsbury in the 1973 Challenge Cup semi-final against Bradford Northern.

DONCASTER
CLUB FORMED IN 1951 - JOINED NORTHERN RUGBY LEAGUE 1951

Club Nostalgia

(Above) Powerful prop KEVIN PARKHOUSE, who is fondly remembered as one of Doncaster's most popular players ever.

(Above) The Doncaster team pictured at Tattersfield in the early 1990s - captained by ex-Great Britain international Kevin Rayne, as well as the long-serving Audley Pennant this team includes a young New Zealander Carl Hall - one of the men behind the revival of the Dons in 2007.

(Left) Programme showing life with the Dons at Tattersfield in 1982 with long-serving player George Pflaster featured on the front cover.

DO YOU KNOW?
Which former Doncaster player has been a coach with the French national team during the last two Rugby Union World Cups?

10 HISTORIC MILESTONES

1951 - 18th August - first game in the Northern Rugby League sees the Dons open with a 10-3 home win over Wakefield Trinity.

1952 - Record crowd set for Doncaster with a 10,000 all-ticket attendance at the York Road greyhound stadium for Cup-tie versus Bradford.

1953 - First game at their new Tattersfield ground on 27th August, a 34-11 loss to Keighley.

1965 - The Dons reach their first final, finishing runners-up to Huddersfield in the Bottom-14 competition after 13-3 defeat at Tattersfield.

1970 - Doncaster draw 4-all with St.Helens in Challenge Cup third round, and thus appear in the draw for the semi-final for the first time before losing in the replay at Knowsley Road.

1980 - Doncaster are featured in the Yorkshire Television documentary *"Another Bloody Sunday."*

1990 - Tattersfield's new floodlights are switched on by Doncaster staging an Under-21 international match between Great Britain and France.

1994 - The Dons greatest year - they win to promotion to the First Division and for a few weeks are top of the table, winning at St.Helens and establishing a Tattersfield record crowd of 6,017.

1995 - Doncaster goes bust and drop out of the league, but supporters form a new club called the Dragons playing at Meadow Court in Stainforth.

2007 - After seven years playing at Doncaster Rovers' Belle Vue ground, the newly named Lakers become joint tenants of the new Keepmoat Stadium - and have to overcome another crisis - fans step in to save them.

FEATHERSTONE
CLUB FORMED IN 1908 - JOINED NORTHERN UNION 1921

Club Nostalgia

This Featherstone Rovers team was pictred on 23rd August, 1963 before a 17-13 win against Halifax at Thrum Hall. Left to right: *(Standing):* Terry Ramshaw, Tony Lynch, Malcolm Dixon, Arnie Morgan, Eric Broom, Gary Jordan, Ivor Lingard. *(In front):* Keith Cotton, Jack Fennell, Don Fox, Walt Ward, Stan Nicholson and Gary Waterworth.

10 HISTORIC MILESTONES

1921 - 27th August - first game in the Northern Union as Featherstone win 17-3 at Bradford.

1928 - In just their sixth season as a senior club, Featherstone Rovers reach the Championship Final, but are runners-up to Swinton at Oldham.

1940 - Rovers win the Yorkshire Cup, their first major honour, beating Wakefeld 12-9 in the Final.

1952 - Featherstone go to Wembley for the first time, captained by Eric Batten, but lose in the Challenge Cup Final to Workington Town 18-10.

1959 - Record attendance set at Post Office Road with 17,531 crowd versus St.Helens.

1959 - Featherstone win the Yorkshire Cup for the second time, captained by Joe Mullaney, they beat Hull 15-14 in the Final at Odsal Stadium.

1967 - Rovers win the Challenge Cup for the first time, skipper Malcolm Dixon receives the Cup from H.M. the Queen after 17-12 Wembley win over Barrow. Carl Dooler wins Lance Todd Trophy.

1973 - Second Wembley win as Featherstone beat Bradford 33-14 - John Newlove is Rovers capatin and Steve Nash wins Lance Todd Trophy.

1977 - Featherstone win the Rugby League Championship for the only time, as led by Vince Farrar they finish top of the First Division.

1983 - Rovers cause an upset at Wembley to beat Hull 14-12 and win the Challenge Cup for a third time. David Hobbs win Lance Todd Trophy.

(Above) PETER SMITH gets a perfect pass away to full-back NIGEL BARKER as Featherstone Rovers beat Hull to win the Challenge Cup at Wembley in 1983. Rovers prop MICK GIBBINS looks on and the Hull man is ex-Featherstone player Charlie Stone.

DO YOU KNOW?
Who was the last man to coach Featherstone Rovers to victory at Wembley in a Challenge Cup Final?

HALIFAX
CLUB FORMED IN 1873 - NORTHERN UNION FOUNDER MEMBER 1895

Club Nostalgia

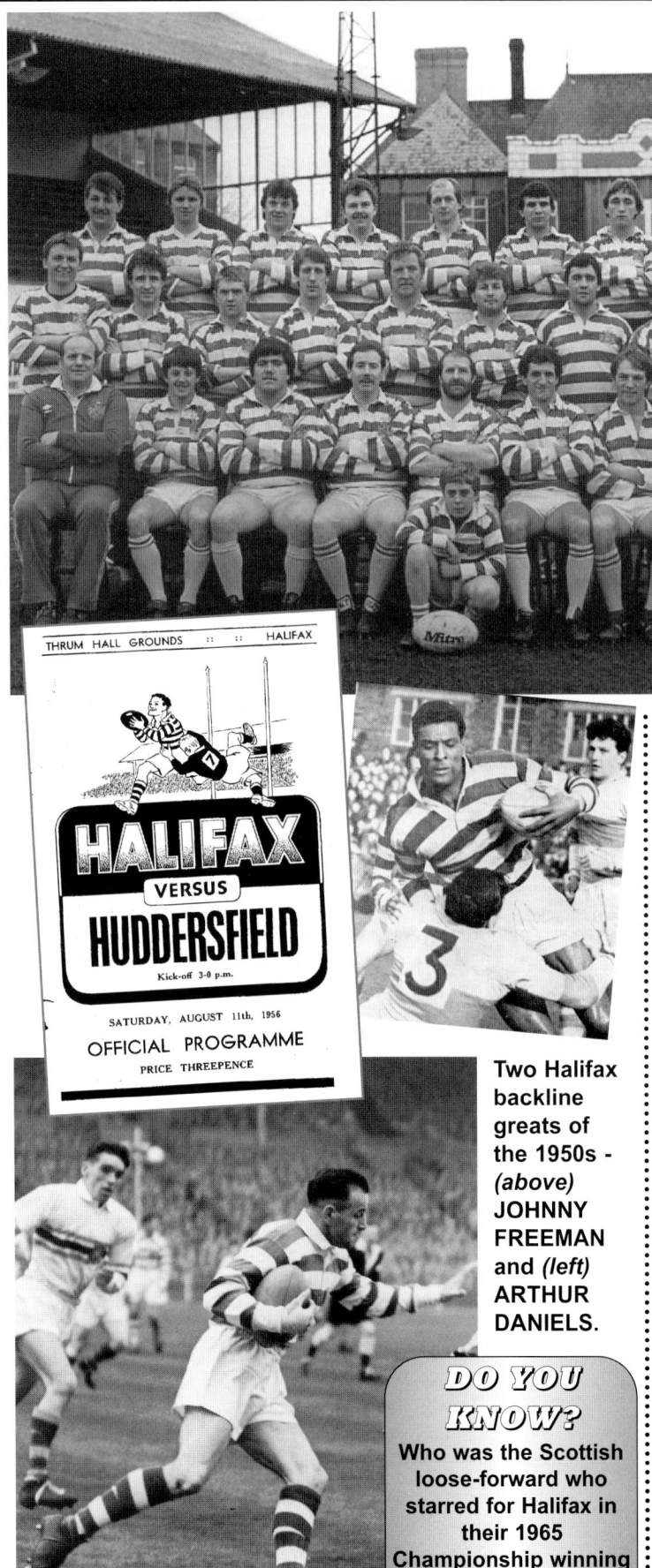

The Halifax squad at Thrum Hall in the mid-1980s, in the days when former star forwards Colin Dixon and Jack Scroby were the coaches. This was the era just before the arrival of player-coach Chris Anderson and his troops from Australia brought some glory days back to Halifax.

Two Halifax backline greats of the 1950s - *(above)* JOHNNY FREEMAN and *(left)* ARTHUR DANIELS.

10 HISTORIC MILESTONES

1895 - 7th September - first game in Northern Union, Halifax win at Liversedge 5-nil

1903 - Halifax win the double, taking both the Championship and Challenge Cup, the latter after beating Salford 7-nil in the Final at Headingley.

1931 - First Wembley Final for Halifax and they beat York 22-8 to win the Challenge Cup.

1939 - Wembley glory again - inspired by full-back Hubert Lockwood Halifax beat favourites Salford 20-3 to win the Challenge Cup Final.

1954 - Halifax are runners-up in both Cup and Championship Finals, and take part in the famous Odsal replay in front of a world record crowd.

1959 - A record attendance is set at Thrum Hall when 29,153 watch a cup-tie against Wigan.

1965 - Captained by John Burnett, 'Fax beat St.Helens in the Final to become Rugby League Champions for the first time since 1907.

1986 - Halifax win the Championship, after a remarkable revival inspired by Australian player-coach Chris Anderson.

1987 - Crowning glory for their president David Brook as Chris Anderson leads 'Fax to the Challenge Cup, beating St.Helens 19-18 in one of Wembley's most dramatic Finals. Graham Eadie wins the Lance Todd Trophy.

1998 - Halifax leave Thrum Hall after over 100 years and move in with Halifax Town at The Shay.

DO YOU KNOW?
Who was the Scottish loose-forward who starred for Halifax in their 1965 Championship winning season?

HARLEQUINS

CLUB FORMED IN 1980 AS FULHAM - JOINED RUGBY LEAGUE 1980

Club Nostalgia

The original Fulham team pictured at Craven Cottage just before their roller-coaster adventure of keeping a professional Rugby League club in London began in September, 1980. Pictured are, left to right, *(Standing):* George Noyce (club secretary), Tony Kinsey, David Hull, Tony Gourley, Ian van Bellen, John Wood, David Allen, Roy Lester, David Eckersley. *(Seated):* Malcolm MacDonald (Fulham director), Mal Aspey, Reg Bowden (Player-coach), Ernie Clay (club chairman), Tony Karalius (Captain), Harold Genders (Director), Derek Noonan, Adrian Cambriani and Colin Welland (Director).

(Above) DAVID HULL, one of the outstanding players in the first season of Fulham- 1980-81.

10 HISTORIC MILESTONES

1980 - 14th September - first game in Rugby League as Fulham, player-coached by Reg Bowden, beat Wigan 24-5 at Craven Cottage.
1981 - A club record attendance is set as 15,013 watch cup-tie with Wakefield at Craven Cottage.
1984 - The original Fulham club, formed by the Football Club, is wound up but a new Fulham is formed by Roy and Barbara Close and play at Crystal Palace National Sports Centre.
1985 - Fulham set up home at the Polytechnic Stadium in Chiswick where they stay for 5 years.
1991 - Fulham join forces with York to make a pioneering tour to Russia.
1991 - The club name is changed to London Crusaders, in 1993 they move to Barnet Copthall Stadium and a year later play in the Division Premiership Final at Old Trafford v. Workington.
1994 - The club is bought by the Brisbane Broncos and is renamed London Broncos.
1996 - Allocated a place in the new Super League, London Broncos play at Charlton's The Valley. 9,000 watch first match there versus Paris.
1999 - A year after Richard Branson becomes club Chairman, London Broncos reach the Challenge Cup Final, losing to Leeds in the last Final to be staged at the old Wembley stadium.
2006 - The club cease to be the Broncos, stop playing at Brentford and move back to the Stoop to play under the banner of Harlequins.

(Above) HUSSAIN M'BARKI on the ball for Fulham against Wigan at Central Park in 1981-82 as Henderson Gill gives chase and the Londoners' stand-off, JOHN CROSSLEY, looks to give support. M'Barki will always be remembered as one the Fulham favourites, a man symbolic with the fun of the London club's early years.

DO YOU KNOW?
Who were the R.L. Champions whom Fulham beat in a special challenge match at Craven Cottage in May, 1981?

48

HUDDERSFIELD
CLUB FORMED IN 1864 - NORTHERN UNION FOUNDER MEMBER 1895

Club Nostalgia

Huddersfield's team of all nationalities in 1949 as a glorious Fartown era was underway. They are, left to right: *(Standing):* Jim Bowden, Lionel Cooper, Jack Maiden, John Daly, Dave Valentine, Hughes, Mel Meek. *(In front):* Ferguson, Hilton, Bob Nicholson, Jeff Bawden (Captain), Billy Banks and George "Happy" Wilson. Missing from the line-up on this occasion were the Australian favourites Pat Devery and Johnny Hunter.

(Above) Fartown's "SPANKY" DYSON, long-serving full-back and prolific goal-kicker. *(Left)* PETER RAMSDEN pictured diving over for his try at Wembley in the 1962 Cup Final, with Wakefield's full-back Gerry Round on his back. Ramsden was one of the first local boys to break into the great Fartown side which won the Cup at Wembley in 1953 when he was the Lance Todd Trophy winner at the age of 19.

10 HISTORIC MILESTONES

1895 - 14th September - first game in Northern Union, Huddersfield beat Wakefeld Trinity 10-nil.

1906 - Harold Wagstaff, the original "Prince of Centres" and one of Fartown's greatest legends, makes his debut for Huddersfield at the age of 15

1915 - Huddersfield's famous "Team of All Talents" become only the second club in the game's history to win the coveted "All Four Cups."

1922 - The game's very first Supporters' Club is founded by the followers of Fartown.

1933 - Huddersfield win the Challenge Cup in their first appearance at Wembley, beating Warrington 21-17 in a thrilling Final.

1950 - Record attendance set at Fartown as 32,912 watch Huddersfield match versus Wigan.

1953 - Captained by Russ Pepperell, and with 19-year-old local lad Peter Ramsden winning the Lance Todd Trophy, Huddersfield put the seal on a great post-war era by winning the Challenge Cup at Wembley again, beating St.Helens 15-10.

1962 - Huddersfield win the last Rugby League Championship to be decided under the old top-four system - captained by Tommy Smales they beat Wakefield in the Final at Odsal just a week after losing to Trinity in the Challenge Cup Final at Wembley.

1994 - Having vacated Fartown and played at the Leeds Road football ground, Huddersfield make their debut at the new McAlpine Stadium.

2006 - Huddersfield reach their first Challenge Cup Final in 44 years, this time at Twickenham.

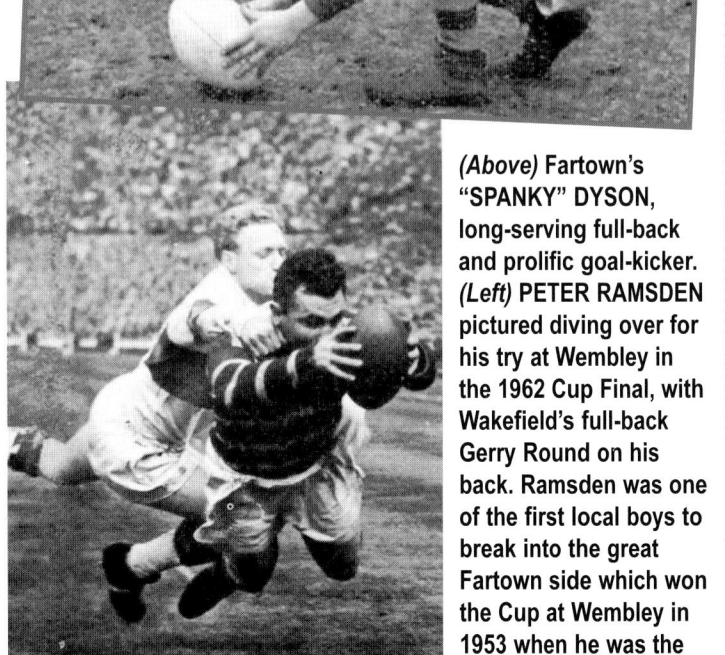

DO YOU KNOW?
Who was Huddersfield's Cumbrian forward who was a member of the 1946 "Indomitables" touring team?

HULL

CLUB FORMED IN 1865 - NORTHERN UNION FOUNDER MEMBER 1895

Club Nostalgia

(Above) Experienced full-back COLIN HUTTON (third from the left) has some words of encouragement for this Hull "A" team before they took the field in November 1957. It was Hutton's last minute goal which won the 1956 Championship Final for Hull.

10 HISTORIC MILESTONES

1895 - 7th September first game in Northern Union, Hull lose away at Batley 7-3.

1913 - The legendary Billy Batten signs for Hull and marks his debut with try hat-trick.

1914 - Hull win the Challenge Cup for the first time, beating Wakefield Trinity 6-nil in the Final.

1936 - Record attendance set at the Boulevard as 28,798 watch cup-tie between Hull and Leeds.

1950 - Johnny Whiteley, who was to become one of Hull's most famous players and revered captains, makes his debut for the Airlie Birds.

1956 - Hull win the Championship after a 10-9 Final victory over Halifax at Maine Road, in which full-back Colin Hutton kicks a last minute penalty goal to snatch the title.

1958 - The Airlie Birds are Rugby League Champions again - in their third successive top-four play-off Final they beat Workington at Odsal.

1982 - Hull win the Challenge Cup for the first time in 68 years - captained by David Topliss they beat Widnes in a replayed Final at Elland Road, Leeds after the teams had drawn at Wembley.

2002 - Hull leave the Boulevard and move into the new Kingston Communications Stadium.

2005 - Hull win the Challenge Cup, beating hot favourites Leeds 25-24 in the Final played in Cardiff.

(Above) ROY'S BOYS - coach Roy Francis leads his Hull team to the Railway Station on their way to play a big match in the 1950s.

This Hull team is from the mid 1960s, captained by Arthur Keegan it includes: Howard Firth, Dick Gemmell, Jim Neale and Clive Sullivan.

DO YOU KNOW?
Who captained Hull in the 1959 and 1960 Wembley Finals?

HULL K.R.
CLUB FORMED IN 1883 - JOINED NORTHERN UNION 1899

Club Nostalgia

Hull Kingston Rovers in the 1962-63 season. Left to right, *(Standing):* Ken Grice, Johnny Williams (masseur), Brian Tyson, Terry Major, John Taylor, P.Murphy, Bob Harris, Allen Lockwood, Harry Poole. *(In front):* Arthur Bunting, Mike Blackmore, David Elliott, Cyril Kellett, Graham Paul, Peter Flanagan, Brian Hatch and Jim Drake.

(Right)
GARY PROHM - the New Zealand international who was such a star with Hull K.R. in their successful years of the 1980s. Equally at home in the pack or centre.

(Left)
Memories of the old Craven Park with the 1971-72 edition of the *"The Robin"* - a big favourite from the Rovers Supporters' Club.

DO YOU KNOW?
Which Cumbrian forward captained Hull K.R. in their successful 1966-67 season

10 HISTORIC MILESTONES

1899 - 2nd September, first game in Northern Union, Hull K.R. lose 3-nil away to Bradford.

1923 - Hull Kingston Rovers win the Championship for the first time, beating Huddersfield 15-5 in the Final.

1925 - The Robins are Champions again, beating Swinton 9-5 in the Final at Rochdale, and they also reach the Challenge Cup Final.

1953 - A record attendance for a Rovers' home match is set when 27,670 watch league match against Hull at Boothferry Park. Back in 1922, the record crowd for Craven Park was set at 22,282.

1964 - Hull K.R. reach Wembley for the first time, captained by Harry Poole they lose the Final 13-5 to Widnes.

1966 - Roger Millward, one of the greatest names in the history of Hull K.R., makes his debut. His career as both player and coach at Rovers would go on to span 25 years.

1968 - A magnificent season for Rovers, in which they won the Yorkshire Cup, ends with them as runners-up to Wakefield in the Championship Final and sending five players, plus coach Colin Hutton, down-under with Britain's World Cup team.

1980 - In the historic all-Humberside Challenge Cup Final, Rovers beat neighbours Hull 10-5 at Wembley.

1985 - Hull K.R. complete back to back Championship titles under coach Roger Millward.

1997 - The Robins claim a unique trophy at Wembley when they win the Challenge Cup Plate, beating Hunslet in the once-only competition.

51

HUNSLET
CLUB FORMED IN 1883 - NORTHERN UNION FOUNDER MEMBER 1895

Club Nostalgia

(Above) Captained by Dickie Williams, the Hunslet team which played Barrow in the 1955 Challenge Cup semi-final.

10 HISTORIC MILESTONES

1895 - 7th September - first game in Northern Union, Hunslet lose at Warrington 5-4.

1908 - Hunslet are the first club to achieve the coveted All Four Cups.

1924 - Record attendance set at Parkside as 24,700 watch Hunslet v Wigan Cup-tie.

1934 - Hunslet reach Wembley Final for the first time and beat Widnes 11-5 to win the Challenge Cup.

1938 - Hunslet win the Championship Final 8-2 against Leeds in front of record 54,112 crowd at Elland Road.

1951 - Geoff Gunney, the most enduring figure in the club history, makes the first of his record 572 appearances.

1959 - Hunslet reach the Championship Final but go down to St.Helens in a epic match at Odsal.

1965 - Hunslet, skippered by Fred Ward and with a X111 containing nine local Hunslet products are gallant runners-up to Wigan, 16-20, in one of Wembley's most memorable Challenge Cup Finals.

1973 - Last ever game at Parkside and the old Hunslet dies - only for a New Hunslet to be formed, led by the loyal Geoff Gunney.

1999 - Now based at the South Leeds stadium, Hunslet win the Northern Ford Premiership Grand Final over Dewsbury at Headingley, but are denied promotion to the Super League.

DO YOU KNOW?
Which Hunslet player shared the Lance Todd Trophy in the 1965 Challenge Cup Final?

(Above) Pictured on the way to Wembley in 1965, Hunslet forward KEN EYRE powers his way through the Wakefield defence, despite Harold Poynton's attempted tackle, in the semi-final win over Trinity at Headingley. In support is Hunslet's other prop DENNIS HARTLEY.

(Above) GEOFF GUNNEY, a man who gave a lifetime of service to the Hunslet club as player and official, pictured diving over for a try against Bradford Northern at Odsal. The other Hunslet player supporting Gunney is Brian Shaw.

KEIGHLEY
CLUB FORMED IN 1876 - JOINED NORTHERN UNION 1901

Club Nostalgia

The Keighley team pictured in August, 1964. Left to right: *(Standing):* Bill Aspinall, Dave Worthy, Albert Bloomfield, Frank Haigh, Tony Walsh, Brian Gaines, Mel Smith, Albert Eyre, Dlambulo. *(In front):* Dave Wilmot, Terry O'Brien, Garfield Owen, Roy Sabine, Alan Edwards and Dave Biltcliffe.

(Above) **PETER ROE** pictured in the Keighley team in 1974 - Peter has gone on to give a lifetime of service to the game, as player and coach.

JOHN WASYLIZ - played for Keighley for just three seasons in the early '90s, but he set records as a prolific points-scorer.

DO YOU KNOW?
Who was the Keighley Cougars coach when they won the Second Division Premiership Final in 1995?

10 HISTORIC MILESTONES

1901 - 7th September - first game in Northern Union as Keighley win away at Bramley 9-2.

1937 - Keighley play at Wembley in the Challenge Cup Final for the first and only time in their history, but are beaten by Widnes.

1951 - A record attendance of 14,500 set at Lawkholme Lane for Cup-tie versus Halifax.

1951 - Keighley reach the Yorkshire Cup Final, finishing runners-up 3-17 to Wakefield Trinity in front of over 25,000 people at Fartown.

1955 - Winger Terry Hollindrake becomes the first Keighley player to represent Great Britain in a Test match, against New Zealand at Headingley.

1961 - The Lawkholme Lane ground is bought by the club from the Duke of Devonshire's estate.

1976 - Keighley go within a whisker of Wembley, as they lose 5-4 to St.Helens in the Challenge Cup semi-final.

1977 - Prolific goal-kicker Brian Jefferson retires after a momentous career with Keighley which spanned 300 games in 12 years, and saw him play for both Yorkshire and England.

1991 - Everything changed as Keighley became the Cougars and a whole new era of razzmatazz, big crowds and headline-grabbing success began.

1995 - Keighley are crowned Second Division Champions and win the Premiership Final at Old Trafford 26-6 over Huddersfield, only to be denied promotion in controversial circumstances due to the advent of the new Super League.

LEEDS

CLUB FORMED IN 1890 - NORTHERN UNION FOUNDER MEMBER 1895

Club Nostalgia

10 HISTORIC MILESTONES

Leeds team before playing a Lazenby Cup match at Hunslet in August 1964. Left to right, *(Standing):* Mick Joyce, Louis Neumann, Towler, John Davies, Bill Drake, Mick Shoebottom, Thomas, Geoff Wriglesworth, Drew Broatch. *(In front):* Barry Seabourne, Les Chamberlain, Dick Gemmell, Alan Smith, Trevor Oldroyd and Robin Dewhurst.

(Right) The much missed MICK SHOEBOTTOM, in action for Leeds in the 1970 Championship Final against St.Helens at Odsal. The referee is Billy Thompson. Shoebottom was one of five Leeds players that year - along with Syd Hynes, John Atkinson, Alan Smith and Barry Seabourne - to go on the triumphant Lions tour.

(Left) All smiles at Headingley when Leeds captain David Ward lifted the Yorkshire Cup in 1976 - alongside happy team-mates Les Dyl and Roy Dickinson. The Loiners won the Yorkshire Cup 17 times in all, notably six times during the 1970s when David Ward emerged as a very successful and popular leader.

DO YOU KNOW?
Who holds the Leeds club record for scoring most tries in a season, and what was his famous nickname?

1895 - 7th September - first game in Northern Union, Leeds win away at Leigh 6-3.
1908 - The first Test match in Rugby League history is played at Headingley as the Northern Union (England) beat the All Golds (New Zealand) 14-6.
1921 - Leeds establish a landmark when they pay the game's first £1,000 transfer-fee to sign Harold Buck from Hunslet.
1936 - Leeds go to Wembley for the first time and, captained by Jim Brough, beat Warrington 18-2 to win the Challenge Cup for the fourth time.
1947 - Record attendance set at Headingley when a 40,175 crowd watch league match between Leeds and Bradford Northern.
1957 - The Loiners return to Wembley and win the Cup, beating Barrow 9-7. Scrum-half Jeff Stevenson is first Leeds player to win the Lance Todd Trophy.
1961 - The "Holy Grail" for Leeds is finally achieved as they win the Championship title for the first time in their history. Captained by Lewis Jones and coached by Joe Warham, they beat Warrington 25-10 in the Final played at Odsal.
1968 - Leeds win the famous "Watersplash" Wembley Final, 11-10 against Wakefield Trinity.
1978 - Under the captaincy of David Ward and with Leeds greats like John Holmes and John Atkinson in the backs, the Loiners win their second successive Challenge Cup Final, beating St.Helens 14-12 in a Wembley epic.
1999 - Leeds become the last team to win the Challenge Cup at the old Wembley Stadium, beating London Broncos by a record score of 52-16.

LEIGH

CLUB FORMED IN 1878 - NORTHERN UNION FOUNDER MEMBER 1895

Club Nostalgia

10 HISTORIC MILESTONES

1895 - 7th September - first game in Northern Union, Leigh are beaten 6-3 at home to Leeds.

1906 - Leigh win the Championship for the first time.

1921 - Leigh win the Challenge Cup for the first time, beating Halifax 13-nil in the Final.

1947 - The first game is played at the club's new ground Kirkhall Lane, which was later to be renamed Hilton Park in 1959.

1953 - Leigh's record attendance is set as a crowd of 31,326 pack Kirkhall Lane to watch a cup-tie against St.Helens.

1953 - The sporting world is shocked as Leigh sign world-record breaking sprint star McDonald Bailey - a crowd of 14,996 watch his debut in a December friendly under floodlights at Hilton Park, but it proves to be his one and only game.

1964 - A full Test match is staged at Leigh for the only time as Great Britain thrash France 39-nil.

1971 - The greatest moment in Leigh's history as they go to Wembley for the only time and win the Cup - under the leadership of player-coach Alex Murphy they crush favourites Leeds 24-7.

1981 - Leigh win the Lancashire Cup for the last time, beating Widnes 8-3 in the Final.

1982 - With Alex Murphy back as coach and local hero John Woods as captain, Leigh win the Rugby League Championship for only the second time in their history

(Above) Leigh's most glorious day at Wembley in 1971. The players on the picture are, left to right: *(Standing):* Joe Walsh, Paul Grimes, Stan Dorrington (hidden), Roy Lester, Derek Watts, Jim Fidler, Geoff Clarkson, Mick Collins. *(In front):* Stuart Ferguson, Tony Barrow (hidden), Alex Murphy, David Eckersley, Les Chisnall and Kevin Ashcroft. Leigh had just hammered Leeds to win the Cup.

(Above) CHARLIE PAWSEY - one of Leigh's all-time greats in the 1950s. Tough forward Charlie won 7 G.B. Test caps

Leigh had a unqiue double at the time when they had players chosen to captain both England and Wales in the 1969 European Championship. *(Pictured left)* the Leigh captains were Alex Murphy and Gordon Lewis.

DO YOU KNOW?
Who was the Rugby Union England and British Lions player who signed for Leigh in 1961?

55

LIVERPOOL
CLUB FORMED IN 1902 - JOINED NORTHERN UNION 1922

Club Nostalgia

This was the Liverpool City team which played the Australians at Knotty Ash in the opening match of the 1956 Kangaroo tour. City lost 40-12 in front of a crowd of 4,712. The City team is: left to right: *(Standing)*: F.Greenhough, B.Walsh, Les Hockenhull, G.Crosby, Oliver Teggin, R.Brown, G.Curran. *(In front)*: Ike Fishwick, J.Pearson, J.Wood, W.Parkes, Wilf Hunt and Ray Ashby.

10 HISTORIC MILESTONES

1902 - The club originates as Highfield, a junior team in the Pemberton area of Wigan and four years later becomes known as Wigan Highfield.

1922 - Wigan Highfield become a senior club and play their first game at Tunstall Lane where a crowd of 18,000 sees them beaten 25-10 by Wigan.

1933 - The club is transferred to the capital city and becomes London Highfield, playing matches under floodlights at the White City Stadium.

1934 - After one relatively successful season in London, the club is relocated to Liverpool and is named Liverpool Stanley.

1936 - Liverpool Stanley win the Lancashire League and a ground record attendance of 14,000 is set for their home Championship semi-final against Widnes, which Stanley lose 10-9.

1950 - Stanley move to Knotty Ash and on 26th August lose their first match at their new home to St.Helens.

1951 - The club changes its name to Liverpool City and adopts the green and white colours.

1964 - Full-back Ray Ashby becomes the first and only Liverpool City player to represent Great Britain in a Test match when he plays against France.

1968 - The club is changed into Huyton and move to their purpose built stadium at Alt Park in 1969.

1984 - Huyton move to become Runcorn Highfield and begin a long and winding road that leads through various guises to their eventual demise as Prescot Panthers in 1997.

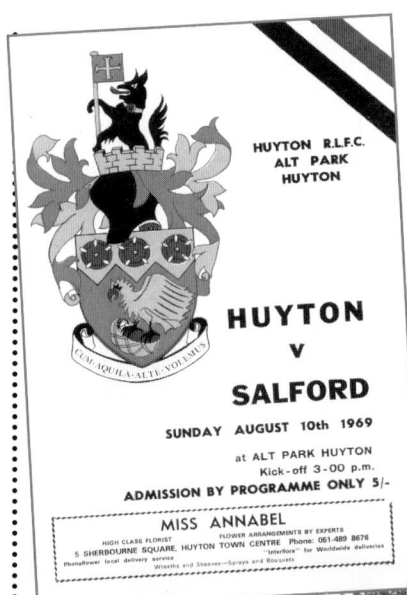

HUYTON R.L.F.C.
ALT PARK
HUYTON

HUYTON v SALFORD

SUNDAY AUGUST 10th 1969
at ALT PARK HUYTON
Kick-off 3-00 p.m.
ADMISSION BY PROGRAMME ONLY 5/-

MISS ANNABEL
HIGH CLASS FLORIST — FLOWER ARRANGEMENTS BY EXPERTS
5 SHERBOURNE SQUARE, HUYTON TOWN CENTRE Phone: 051-489 8676
Phoneflower local delivery service — "Interflora" for Worldwide deliveries
Wreaths and Sheaves—Sprays and Bouquets

DO YOU KNOW?
Which former leading referee played full-back for Huyton?

(Left) Programme for the new Huyton club's debut match at their purpose built Alt Park Stadium. It was Sunday, 10th August 1969 and Salford were the first visitors to Huyton as the name of Liverpool City was no more.

HUYTON - a team group pictured at Halifax in 1983, captained by Alan Bishop (in the middle of the front-row) - brother of Tommy.

OLDHAM
CLUB FORMED IN 1876 - NORTHERN UNION FOUNDER MEMBER 1895

Club Nostalgia

10 HISTORIC MILESTONES

1895 - 14th September - first game in Northern Union, Oldham are beaten 16-8 away at Hunslet.

1899 - Oldham become the first Lancashire side to win the Challenge Cup, beating Hunslet in the Final.

1905 - Oldham win the Championship for the first time, a feat they go on to repeat in the consecutive years of 1910 and 1911, captained by their mighty forward Joe Ferguson.

1927 - Oldham play in their fourth consecutive Challenge Cup Final, and beat Swinton at Wigan to take the trophy.

1949 - Bryn Goldswain signs for Oldham and becomes one of the most influential figures in the emergence of their great team of the 1950s.

1957 - Oldham win the Championship, beating Hull 15-14 in a thrilling Final at Odsal Stadium.

1958 - The Roughyeds complete a hat-trick of Lancashire Cup Final triumphs.

1964 - More Challenge Cup heartache for the club so unlucky never to play at Wembley as Oldham lose to Hull K.R. in the semi-final second replay - after leading in tje first replay only for it to be abandoned due to bad light.

1988 - Oldham win the Division Two Championship and then the Premiership Final at Old Trafford.

1997 - After playing their last game at the Watersheddings, Oldham finish in relegation position from Super League but the club goes into liquidation. A new Oldham club is formed.

(Above) It's a rare action photo that manages to include no less than nine members of one team together - this was Oldham playing Barrow at Watersheddings in 1964. The Oldham players on the floor are John Donovan and Vince Nestor, whilst looking on are: Pyecroft, Whitehead, Parker, McIntyre, Robinson, Wilson, Smethurst, Lord and Simms.
(Left) Oldham captain, the Australian Mal Graham, lifts the Second Division Championship trophy in 1988.

DO YOU KNOW?
Who was the Oldham goal-kicking full-back of the 1950s who went on to become a TV presenter?

The Oldham team in 1965-66. Left to right: *(Standing):* Len McIntyre, "Tug" Wilson, Stuart Whitehead, Alf Mumberson, Jim McCormack, John Winton, Geoff Fletcher. *(Seated):* Brian Lord, Trevor Simms, Dave Parker, John Donovan, Geoff Sims, Bill Broomhead

ROCHDALE HORNETS

CLUB FORMED IN 1871 - NORTHERN UNION FOUNDER MEMBER 1895

Club Nostalgia

10 HISTORIC MILESTONES

1895 - 7th September - first game in Northern Union, Hornets lose at St.Helens 8-3.

1911 - Rochdale win the Lancashire Cup, captained by international half-back Johnny Baxter they beat Oldham 12-5 in the Final at Broughton.

1919 - Hornets win the Lancashire Cup for the third time, led by Devonian skipper George Prudence they hammer Oldham 22-nil in the Final.

1922 - Rochdale win the Challenge Cup for the only time in their history, beating Hull 10-9 in the Final at Headingley.

1924 - A new Rugby League record attendance is set at the Athletic Grounds, Rochdale, as 41,831 watch the Challenge Cup Final there between Oldham and Wigan.

1958 - Hornets go wtihin two points of going to Wembley as they lose 5-3 to Wigan in their last Challenge Cup semi-final at Swinton. Italian winger Ferdi "Corsi" scores the Rochdale points.

1961 - Rochdale start a trend by signing the first players from Fiji - big winger Joe Levula makes his debut and quickly becomes a favourite.

1971 - Captained by Frank Myler, Hornets win through to the Final of the BBC Floodlit Trophy, where they lose 8-2 against St.Helens

1988 - Hornets play their last game at the Athletic Grounds and move in at Spotland.

1991 - Rochdale reach the Lancashire Cup Final for the last time, where they finish gallant runners-up to St.Helens, 24-14 at Warrington.

DO YOU KNOW?
Which well known Rugby League press reporter used to play on the wing for Rochdale Hornets in the 1970s?

Pictured at the Athletic Grounds, Rochdale Hornets in the 1974-75 season. Left to right: *(Standing):* Tony Pratt, Peter Birchall, Tony Gourley, Tony Cooke, Derek Marsh, Mike Leadbetter, Ray Harris, Les Harris. *(In front):* Albert Hillman, John Butler, David Taylor, Tony Halmshaw, John Hammond, Colin Simkins. The mascot was Nigel Greenwood.

(Above, left) Programme for Hornets' fixture against the 1965 New Zealand touring team, with captains Johnny Noon and Bill Snowden pictured on the front cover. *(Above, right)* WILF ROACH, pictured in the 1957-58 season, was a popular centre-threequarter with Rochdale Hornets in the 'fifties. A native of St.Helens, Wilf had played for Saints before transferring to Rochdale.

58

SALFORD
CLUB FORMED IN 1879 - JOINED NORTHERN UNION 1896

Club Nostalgia

Salford in the 1972-73 season as they built towards their Championship-winning team in the following campaign. Many of these players had been recruited in the "Red Devils" team-building campaign instigated by club Chairman, Mr. Brian Snape. Picured are, left to right, *(Standing):* Johnny Ward, Maurice Richards, Graham Mackay, Tony Colloby, Paul Charlton, Alan Grice, Ellis Devlin. *(In front):* Ken Gill, Doug Davies, Chris Hesketh, David Watkins, Peter Banner and Colin Dixon.

DO YOU KNOW?
Who was the famous manager of Salford who built the original "Red Devils" in the 1930s?

(Right) STEVE NASH, in Salford colours. A tough and talented scrum-half, Nash joined the Red Devils from Featherstone after starring for Great Britain in the 1972 World Cup win and the 1974 Lions tour.

(Left) Salford's match programme became one of the most attractive and innovative in the game during the 1970s - heady days of glamour at the Willows.

10 HISTORIC MILESTONES

1896 - 5th September - first game in Northern Union, Salford lose 10-nil away at Widnes.

1901 - Salford's home at the Willows is opened in December 1901 with a victory over Swinton, before a crowd of 16,981.

1914 - Salford get their first major trophy when they win the Championship, beating Huddersfield 5-3 in the Final at Headingley.

1928 - Lance Todd takes up the post of secretary-manager at the Willows and the most glorious era in the club's history is about to unfold.

1934 - The legend of the "Red Devils" is born as Salford undertake a promotional tour to help build the game in France.

1938 - Salford win the Challenge Cup for the only time in their history, captained by the great Gus Risman they beat Barrow 7-4 at Wembley.

1963 - Brian Snape becomes Chairman of the club and sets about creating a new era of success and glamour for Salford as the new Variety Centre makes the Willows a popular entertainment centre.

1969 - Salford return to Wembley but lose 11-6 to Castleford in the Challenge Cup Final.

1974 - The Red Devils win the Rugby League Championship as flying winger Keith Fielding sets a new club record of 46 tries in the season.

1976 - A second Championship in three years for Salford, captained by Chris Hesketh and coached by Les Bettinson.

SHEFFIELD
CLUB FORMED IN 1984 - JOINED RUGBY LEAGUE 1984

Club Nostalgia

(Above) Sheffield Eagles' debut game versus Rochdale at Owlerton Stadium in 1984 - Vince Farrar is the man with the ball.

10 HISTORIC MILESTONES

1984 - 2nd September, first game in the Rugby League Division Two as Sheffield win 29-10 at home to Rochdale Hornets.

1989 - The Eagles play their last game at their original home Owlerton and begin a nomadic 12 months which sees them play in various towns as well as at Hillsborough and Bramall Lane. They win the Second Division Premiership Final at Old Trafford captained by Daryl Powell.

1990 - Sheffield play their first game in the new Don Valley Stadium, beating Wakefield Trinity 34-6.

1992 - The Eagles return to Old Trafford and win another Second Division Premiership tiltle, this time captained by Mick Cook.

1992 - Sheffield win through to the Yorkshire Cup Final in the competition's last year - but finish runners-up to Wakefield at Elland Road, Leeds.

1996 - Sheffield play in the very first Super League match against Paris Saint Germain. Later the same year, the Eagles founder and driving force Gary Hetherington leaves to join Leeds.

1997 - Attendance record set for an Eagles' home game as 10,603 watch match v Bradford.

1998 - The greatest day in the club's history as they beat Wigan at Wembley 17-8 in one of the biggest ever shocks in a Challenge Cup Final. Mark Aston wins the Lance Todd Trophy.

1999 - The club is controversially merged with Huddersfield - but a new Sheffield Eagles club is formed by Mark Aston and loyal supporters.

2006 - Eagles with the National League Two Grand Final and promotion to League One.

(Right) **SONNY NICKLE**, in action for Sheffield in 1990. A barnstorming back-rower, Nickle was one of the Eagles' best discoveries - signed from Hunslet he went on to become a Great Britain international.

(Left) **MARK ASTON** - the man who has now inherited Gary Hetherington's tag as "Mr. Sheffield Eagles," pictured on the front-cover of *"Open Rugby"* magazine in November 1989 when the Eagles had just beaten new World Club Champions Widnes at Bramall Lane.

DO YOU KNOW?
Who was the first coach of the Sheffield Eagles club when they made their debut in Rugby League in 1984?

ST.HELENS
CLUB FORMED IN 1873 - NORTHERN UNION FOUNDER MEMBER 1895

Club Nostalgia

Wembley glory for Saints in 1966 as Bill Sayer, Cliff Watson, Albert Halsall, Len Killeen and John Mantle run with the Cup.

DO YOU KNOW?
Who captained Saints when they won the Challenge Cup and Super League double in 1996?

St.Helens loves to remember its legends, none more than when Tom Van Vollenhoven has come back to visit from South Africa as this special programme shows *(left)*.

10 HISTORIC MILESTONES

1895 - 7th September - first game in Northern Union, St.Helens beat Rochdale Hornets 8-3.

1897 - St.Helens take part in the inaugural Challenge Cup Final, but lose to Batley at Leeds.

1930 - Saints play in the second Wembley Cup Final but suffer a shock defeat to Widnes.

1949 - Record attendance set at Knowsley Road as 35,695 watch Boxing Day match versus Wigan.

1953 - With the great Jim Sullivan beginning a golden era as coach, St.Helens lose at Wembley to Huddersfield but win the Championship. Captained by Duggie Greenall they beat Halifax in the Maine Road Final.

1956 - For the first time in their history, St.Helens win the Challenge Cup - skipper Alan Prescott leads them to Wembley victory over Halifax. In the same year, the greatest Saint of all - Alex Murphy - signs on at Knowsley Road on his 16th birthday.

1961 - Captained by Vince Karalius, Saints beat the old enemy Wigan at Wembley 12-6 to take the Cup. Dick Huddart wins the Lance Todd Trophy.

1966 - A momentous season as St.Helens win four trophies, led by Alex Murphy.

1996 - Saints are the first winners of the new Super League, and complete a double by beating Bradford at Wembley in the Challenge Cup Final.

2006 - Another glory year as St.Helens win a Cup and League double and then go on to win the World Club Championship against Brisbane.

(Above) Saints hero of the 1950s, centre DUGGIE GREENALL, dives over for a try at Knowsley Road against Oldham.

SWINTON

CLUB FORMED IN 1871 - JOINED NORTHERN UNION 1896

Club Nostalgia

10 HISTORIC MILESTONES

1896 - 5th September - first game in Northern Union, Swinton beat Warington 17-6.

1900 - Swinton win the Challenge Cup for the first time, the famous Jim Valentine captaining them to 16-8 win over Salford in the Final.

1928 - Swinton become only the third - and last - team in the history of the game to win the coveted "All Four Cups" - they are led by Hector Halsall.

1929 - The Station Road ground is opened on 2nd March, 1929 - and a crowd of 22,000 watch Swinton beat Wigan in the opening game. Just a year later Station Road stages its first Test match.

1954 - Ken Gowers makes his debut and goes on to set club records for most appearances, goals and points in a 19-year Lions career.

1963 - Captained by Albert Blan Swinton win the Championship as the game experiments with two divisions in the season of the big freeze.

1964 - The Lions cement their reputation as the team of the "swinging sixties" as they retain the Championship with international backs like Gowers, Stopford and Buckley as their stars.

1969 - After numerous Lancashire Cup Finals as runners-up during the 1960s, Swinton at last win the trophy, beating Leigh 11-2 in the Final at Wigan. Devonian Bob Fleet is the Lions captain.

1987 - Swinton win the inaugral Second Division Premiership, beating Hunslet at Old Trafford.

1992 - The Lions play their last game at Station Road before the famous ground is sold for property development. The team moves to play at Bury Football Club's ground.

Swinton's Championship-winning team in the 1963-64 season. This group includes, left to right: (Standing): John Speed, Harold Bate, Ken Halliwell, Dick Bonser, Ron Morgan, Peter Norburn, Derek Clarke. (Seated): Alan Buckley, Bobby Fleet, George Parkinson, Albert Blan (Captain), John Stopford, Frank Halliwell, Malcolm Cummings. (In front): Bernard McMahon, Cliff Berry (inset) and Ken Gowers.

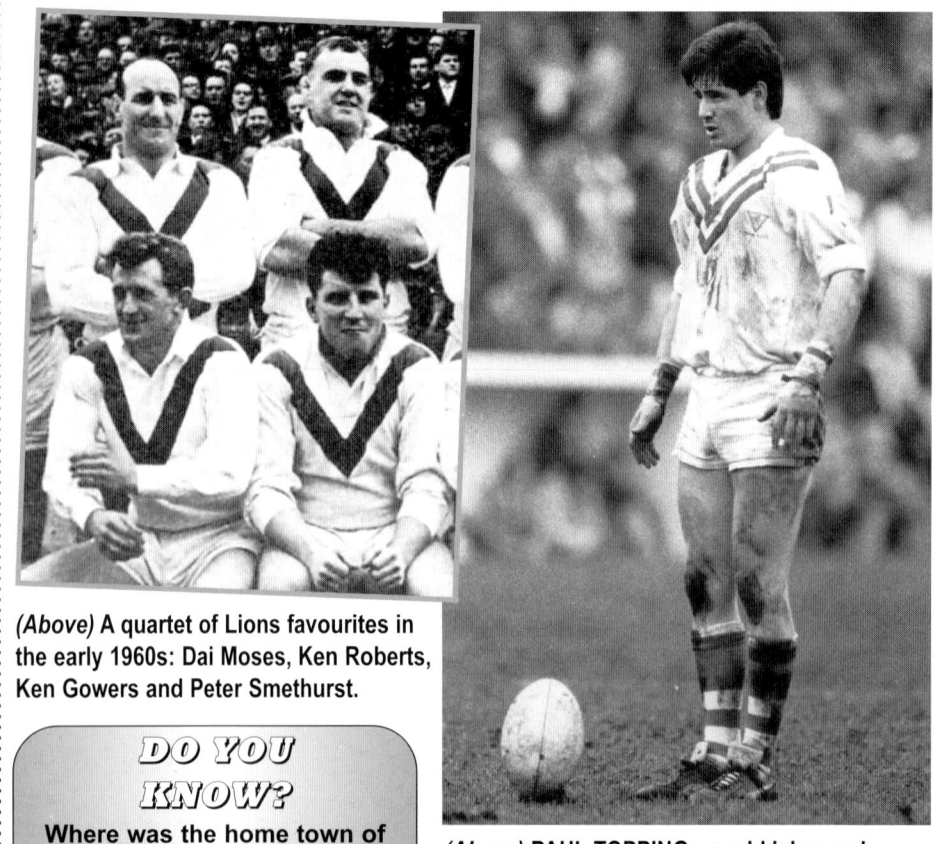

(Above) A quartet of Lions favourites in the early 1960s: Dai Moses, Ken Roberts, Ken Gowers and Peter Smethurst.

DO YOU KNOW?
Where was the home town of Swinton legend Ken Gowers?

(Above) PAUL TOPPING - goal-kicker and good all-rounder for Swinton in the late 1980s.

WAKEFIELD TRINITY

CLUB FORMED IN 1873 - NORTHERN UNION FOUNDER MEMBER 1895

Club Nostalgia

The great Wakefield Trinity team of 1960 with the Challenge Cup and Yorkshire League trophies. Trinity officials are on the back row, and the others pictured are, left to right, *(Second row):* Ken Traill (coach), Albert Firth, Don Vines, Les Chamberlain, Geoff Oakes, Alan Skene, Gerry Round, Jack Wilkinson, Paddy Armour (masseur). *(Front row):* Fred Smith, Neil Fox, Keith Holliday, Mr.Stuart Hadfield (chairman), Derek Turner (captain), Ken Rollin, John Etty and Harold Poynton.

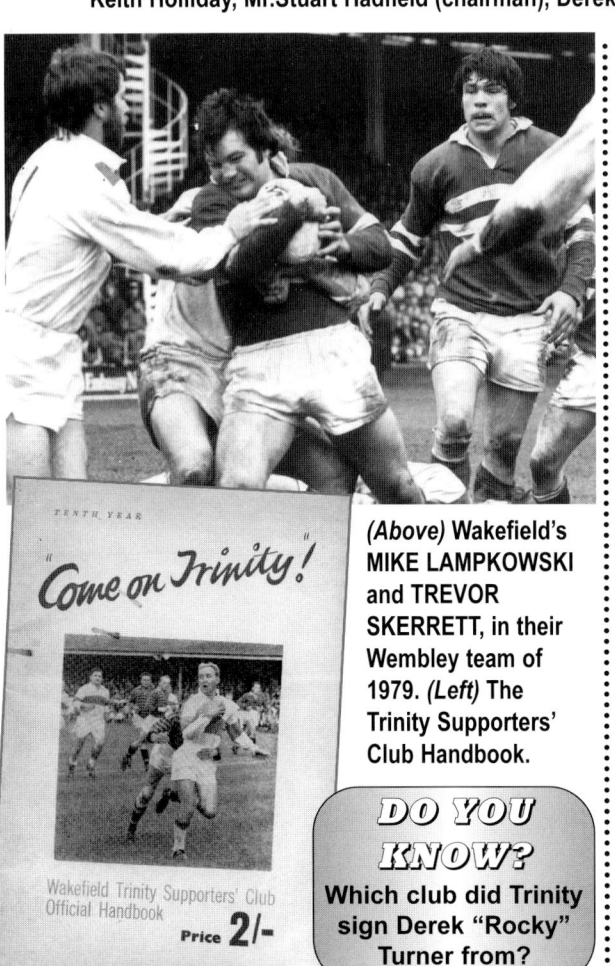

(Above) Wakefield's MIKE LAMPKOWSKI and TREVOR SKERRETT, in their Wembley team of 1979. *(Left)* The Trinity Supporters' Club Handbook.

DO YOU KNOW?
Which club did Trinity sign Derek "Rocky" Turner from?

10 HISTORIC MILESTONES

1895 - 7th September - first game in Northern Union, Wakefield lose 11-nil away at Bradford.

1919 - Trinity win the Challenge Cup for the first time beating Hull 17-nil in the Final at Headingley.

1921 - Record attendance set at Belle Vue as 30,676 watch a cup-tie versus Huddersfield.

1946 - Trinity win the first post-war Cup Final at Wembley beating Wigan 13-12 - their captain Billy Stott becomes the first Lance Todd Trophy winner.

1956 - Wakefield's favourite player, Neil Fox, makes his debut - in a magnificent career he goes on to become the game's greatest points scorer.

1962 - Trinity go within a whisker of winning "All Four Cups" - losing at the last hurdle in the Championship Final against Huddersfield one week after beating them at Wembley to win the Cup.

1963 - Wakefield win the Challenge Cup for the third time in four years as they beat Wigan at Wembley, skipper Derek Turner lifting the trophy on all three occasions.

1967 - Trinity win their "Holy Grail" of the Rugby League Championship trophy, captained by Harold Poynton they beat St.Helens in the Final which went to a midweek replay at Swinton after a draw at Leeds.

1968 - The Championship is retained but Trinity lose the Cup in sensational circumstances to Leeds at Wembley in the "Watersplash Final."

1992 - Wakefield are the last team to win the Yorkshire Cup as they beat Sheffield in the farewell Final.

WARRINGTON
CLUB FORMED IN 1879 - NORTHERN UNION FOUNDER MEMBER 1895

Club Nostalgia

Photo by EDDIE WHITHAM

10 HISTORIC MILESTONES

1895 - 7th September - first game in Northern Union, Warrington beat Hunslet at home 5-4.

1905 - Warrington win the Challenge Cup for the first time beating Hull K.R. in the Final - legendary winger Jackie Fish scores both tries in 6-nil win.

1933 - Warrington reach Wembley for the first time, but they lose in the Final against Huddersfield.

1948 - The Wire win their first Championship as they beat Bradford 15-5 in the Final at Maine Road - captained by Harold Palin.

1950 - Warrington win at Wembley for the first time and Harry Bath becomes the first Australian to captain a Challenge Cup winning team at Wembley as they beat Widnes 19-nil in the Final.

1954 - Warrington achieve a Cup and League double, play in front of a world record crowd in the famous Odsal replay and Gerry Helme becomes the first man to win the Lance Todd Trophy twice.

1962 - Emotional scenes at Wilderspool as Brian Bevan, the greatest try-scorer in the history of the game, makes his farewell appearance for the Wire.

1974 - With Alex Murphy as player-coach, Warrington win the Challenge Cup beating Featherstone at Wembley and go on to win four out of five available major trophies.

1986 - Warrington win the Premiership trophy for the only time, beating Halifax in the Final at Elland Road. Les Boyd wins Harry Sunderland Trophy.

2003 - The club says farewell to their old home at Wilderspool and moves into the brand new Halliwell Jones Stadium.

(Above) Memories of Wilderspool in the late 1970s as Warrington forward TOMMY MARTYN battles against the Blackpool Borough defence. The nearest Wire player in support is scrum-half PARRY GORDON.

DO YOU KNOW?
Which Australian "immortal" and former Kangaroo captain was born in Warrington and played a season for the Wire?

(Right) LES BOYD lifts the Premiership Trophy in 1986 after Warrington's victory over Halifax. Australian forward Boyd was very popular with the Wilderspool fans and had just been awarded the Harry Sunderland Trophy.

The Warrington team in 1953, including on the back row: Ike Fishwick, Jim Featherstone, A.Humphreys, Dan Naughton, S.Phillips, Bob Ryan and E.White. And on the front row: Brian Bevan, Ally Naughton, Cec Mountford (captain) and Gerry Helme.

64

WHITEHAVEN

CLUB FORMED IN 1948 - JOINED NORTHERN RUGBY LEAGUE 1948

Club Nostalgia

The Whitehaven team in 1998. Left to right: *(Standing):* Gary Charlton, Leroy Joe, David Seeds, Colin Armstrong, Graeme Morton, Siose Muliumu, Craig Chambers, Les Quirk, Simon Knox. *(In front):* Peter Smith, Wesley Wilson, David Fatialofa, Aaron Lester (Captain), Lee Kiddie, Graeme Lewthwaite, Kevin Hetherington and Gus Malietoa-Brown.

10 HISTORIC MILESTONES

1948 - 21st August, first game in the Northern Rugby League, Whitehaven beat Hull 5-nil.

1956 - Whitehaven beat the Australian tourists 14-11 in front of an 11,000 crowd.

1957 - Whitehaven, captained by Billy Garratt, go agonisingly close to a Wembley appearance, losing 10-9 to Leeds in the Cup semi-final in front of almost 50,000 at Odsal after a late, controversial drop-goal by Jeff Stevenson.

1958 - Dick Huddart, the club's greatest product, becomes the only Whitehaven player to go on a Lions tour and the first to play Test football.

1960 - Record attendance set at the Recreation Ground as 18,650 crowd watch a Challenge Cup quarter-final against Wakefield Trinity.

1962 - Whitehaven's most famous player, full-back John McKeown, retires after a career which began on the club's foundation day in 1948 and in which he set unbroken records for appearances, goals and points.

1965 - Captained by Test stand-off Phil Kitchin, Whitehaven win a famous victory over the New Zealanders 12-7.

1970 - Whitehaven qualify for the top-16 Championship play-offs for the first time under player-coach Sol Roper and after achieving a shock 20-all draw at Central Park go on to beat Wigan 9-4 win the replay.

2000 - The Whitehaven club is saved by supporters from a forced merger which would have seen them de-camped to Workington.

2005 - Captained by Aaron Lester, Haven win their first senior trophy when they finish as National League One minor premiers - but they go on to lose their second successive Grand Final.

Two of Whitehaven's "Mighty Macs" - *(Inset, above)* BILL McALONE, the prop-forward of the 1950s who Great Britain captain Alan Prescott described as his toughest opponent. *(Above, left)* MATT McLEOD - playing for Whitehaven at Blackpool in 1965. Kells product Matt later signed for Wakefield Trinity and played in the infamous "Watersplash" Final at Wembley.

DO YOU KNOW?
Who was the last Whitehaven player to be capped in a Test match by Great Britain?

WIDNES
CLUB FORMED IN 1873 - NORTHERN UNION FOUNDER MEMBER 1895

Club Nostalgia

"The Chemics" in 1964, the year in which they won the Cup at Wembley. Left to right, *(Standing):* George Kemel, Frank Myler, Edgar Bate, Bob Randall, Wally Hurstfield, Arthur Hughes, Jim Measures, Frank Collier. *(Seated):* Ged Lowe, Alan Briers, Vince Karalius (captain), Bobby Chisnall, Bill Thompson, Johnny Gaydon. *(In front):* Ged Smith and Ray Owen.

10 HISTORIC MILESTONES

1895 - 7th September - first game in Northern Union, Widnes lose 15-4 at neighbours Runcorn.

1930 - Widnes play in the second Wembley Cup Final and with a team of 12 locals plus a South African they cause a huge shock by beating St.Helens to win the trophy for the first time.

1933 - Widnes full-back Jimmy Hoey becomes the first man in the game's history to reach the milestone of scoring in every match in a season.

1937 - The Chemics become the first club to win at Wembley twice as they beat Keighley 18-5 to win the Challenge Cup Final.

1961 - Record attendance set at Naughton Park as 24,205 watch a Cup replay against St.Helens.

1964 - Captained by Vince Karalius Widnes win the Challenge Cup beating Hull K.R. at Wembley.

1975 - The Chemics win at Wembley again, beating Warrington in the Final, as a great era of Widnes success begins. Local lad Ray Dutton kicks his way to the Lance Todd Trophy.

1979 - With scrum-half Reg Bowden as acaptain Widnes win four major trophies, including the Challenge Cup at Wembley.

1984 - The Chemics beat Wigan at Wembley with two spectacular tries from Joe Lydon.

1989 - Widnes win the World Club Challenge by beating Australian champions Canberra Raiders 30-18 in a superb display at Old Trafford.

DO YOU KNOW?
Who was the Widnes coach when they won the World Club Challenge in 1989?

(Right) MICK ADAMS lifts the Premiership trophy for Widnes in 1982. Adams had a great career as a key footballer in the great Chemics era of success from the mid-1970s onwards.

Widnes celebrate getting to Wembley in 1975. Along with coaches Vince Karalius and Harry Dawson, players in the picture include: Jim Mills, Reg Bowden, Keith Elwell, Barry Sheridan, Alan Prescott, John Foran, Mal Aspey and Mick George.

WIGAN
CLUB FORMED IN 1879 - NORTHERN UNION FOUNDER MEMBER 1895

Club Nostalgia

In 1959 Wigan became the first team to win two successive Wembley Finals when they beat Hull at the Empire Stadium. Many more Wembley triumphs were to follow for the men in cherry and white.
The victorious Wigan team of 1959, chairing their skipper Eric Ashton with the Cup, is, left to right: *(Standing):* Brian McTigue, Rees Thomas, John Barton, Mick Sullivan, Bill Bretherton, Bill Sayer, Billy Boston, Roy Evans. *(In front):* Keith Holden, Fred Griffiths, Norman Cherrington and David Bolton.

DO YOU KNOW?
Who captained Wigan to their first Wembley Cup Final win of the 1980s?

(Right) Wigan's most decorated player SHAUN EDWARDS, a star of the 1980s and early '90s at Central Park.

(Left) Wigan programme from 1975-76 with Test forward BOB IRVING (formerly with Oldham) pictured scoring a try on the front cover.

10 HISTORIC MILESTONES

1895 - 7th September - first game in Northern Union, Wigan win 9-nil at Broughton Rangers.
1902 - Central Park is opened on 6th September as Wigan's first match there is against Batley.
1924 - Wigan the Challenge Cup for the first time beating Oldham 21-4 in the Final.
1929 - Wigan play in the very first Wembley Final and, captained by the great Jim Sullivan, beat Dewsbury 13-2 to win the Challenge Cup.
1950 - In an amazing achievement, despite missing eight international players on tour with the Lions, Wigan beat Huddersfield 20-2 to win the Championship Final at Maine Road.
1953 - Billy Boston, Wigan's most famous player, is signed and makes his Central Park debut, scoring a try versus Barrow.
1959 - Record attendance set at Central Park as 47,477 watch league fixture against Saints.
1987 - Wigan win the World Club Challenge by beating Aussie champions Manly 8-2 on a night of electric atmosphere at Central Park
1995 - Wigan take the game's records to new limits as they win their eighth consecutive Challenge Cup and sixth successive Cup and League double.
1999 - Beset by financial problems, Wigan are forced to sell their famous home at Central Park and watch it rapidly become a supermarket.

67

WORKINGTON TOWN
CLUB FORMED IN 1945 - JOINED NORTHERN RUGBY LEAGUE 1945

Club Nostalgia

10 HISTORIC MILESTONES

1945 - 25th August, first game in the Northern Rugby League as Workington beat Broughton Rangers 27-5 at Borough Park.

1946 - A defining moment in the history of the club as Gus Risman is appointed player-manager on his return from captaining the 1946 tourists.

1951 - Workington win the Championship as they beat Warrington 26-11 in the Final at Maine Road.

1952 - Just seven years after their formation Town win the game's other major trophy when they beat Featherstone 18-10 at Wembley. The majestic Gus Risman proudly lifts the Cup.

1955 - Now coached by Jim Brough, Workington go back to Wembley but are beaten by north-west neighbours Barrow in the Challenge Cup Final.

1956 - Town leave Borough Park and move into their new purpose built stadium at Derwent Park.

1958 - Workington reach their third Wembley Final in six years and also the Championship Final - but, badly hit by injuries in both games, finish runners-up to Wigan and Hull. Four Town players, plus coach Brough and manager Tom Mitchell, go with the Great Britain touring team to Australia.

1962 - Workington win the new Western Championship, beating Widnes 10-nil in a replayed Final at Wigan - Brian Edgar captains Town.

1965 - Record attendance set at Derwent Park as 17,741 watch Challenge Cup match versus Wigan.

1977 - Workington win the Lancashire Cup, captained by Paul Charlton, they beat Wigan in the Final at Warrington.

This Workington Town team pictured at the start of the 1962-63 season. Left to right: *(Standing):* Billy Ivison (Coach), Danny Gardiner, Bill Martin, Matt McLeod, Malcolm Moss, Tom McNally, John O'Neill, W. Miller (Assistant coach). *(Seated):* John Short (physio), Japie Ferreira, Harry Archer, Brian Edgar (Captain), Sol Roper, Piet Pretorious, John Wilson (skipman). *(In front):* Benny Eve and Syd Lowden.

BILLY IVISON - EPPIE GIBSON - JIMMY HAYTON
Three of the 'greats' in Workington's history

DO YOU KNOW?
Who was the Workington Town player who captained Great Britain in all three Tests of the 1966 Ashes series in Australia?

Bill Pattinson celebrates as Workington captain Paul Charlton lifts the Lancashire Cup after victory over Wigan in the 1977 Final. A happy Chairman George Graham looks on.

68

YORK

CLUB FORMED IN 1868 - JOINED NORTHERN UNION 1898

Club Nostalgia

(Left) The York team in the 1974-75 season captained by the much travelled Great Britain international forward Terry Clawson.
They are, left to right, *(Standing):* Gary Hetherington, Steve Quinn, Barry Andrews, Gary Smith, Charlie Hillman, Peter Cookland, Ron Wileman, Colin Wood. *(In front):* David Barends, Danny Sheehan, Keith Taylor, Tony Handforth, Terry Clawson, Adrian Rushton and Terry Day.

(Right) GARY STEPHENS - the former Castleford, Wigan and Great Britain scrum-half, pictured in the York colours in the late 1980s. Stephens went on to coach York including on their pioneering tour to Russia alongside Fulham in 1991.

(Left) MICK SULLIVAN in action for York in the early 1960s at Clarence Street versus Hull. Centre Dick Gemmell is the Hull player trying to tackle him. Sullivan, Great Britain's most capped international, played for York from the 1961-62 season until the 1964-65 season, and won his last Test cap as a York player when he appeared against Australia in the Swinton Test of the 1963 Ashes series.

10 HISTORIC MILESTONES

1898 - York make their Northern Union debut as a junior club, and play their first game as a senior club against Goole on 7th September 1901.

1922 - York win the Yorkshire Cup for the first time, captained by Welshman Joe Corsi they beat Batley 5-nil in front of 33,719 at Headingley.

1931 - York go to Wembley for the only time in their history, but lose an entertaining Cup Final to Halifax 22-8. Billy Thomas is York's captain.

1936 - York win the Yorkshire Cup for the third time beating Wakefield 9-2 in the Final at Leeds.

1954 - Local lad Basil Watts is called up for the inaugural World Cup tournament in France and plays in the second-row in all four games as Great Britain become the first rugby World Cup winners.

1959 - York's Jeff Stevenson becomes the last man to captain Great Britain to an Ashes series victory against Australia on home soil.

1984 - York go so close to a second Wembley appearance - after a great Cup run in which Graham Steadman stars, they are most unlucky to lose to Wigan 14-8 in the semi-final played at Elland Road.

1989 - The club plays its last match at the Clarence Street ground set in the shadows of York Minster, and moves to a new stadium out of town at Monks Cross, adopting the name Ryedale-York.

1991 - York join forces with Fulham to make a pioneering tour to Russia.

2002 - The original York club, in financial difficulty, is wound up and "the Wasps" are no more. But a new club is soon formed as the York City Knights.

DO YOU KNOW?
Who was the appropriately named player who set the York club record for most goals and points in a career?

69

GREAT BRITAIN GALLERY

Remember these players who all wore the Great Brtain colours with distinction in Test matches, World Cups and on Lions tours - including some of our nation's most inspirational sporting captains.

Dickie Williams	*Frank Myler*	*Jack Grundy*	*Ted Cahill*	*Phil Lowe*
Tommy Harris	*Arnold Morgan*	*Brian Briggs*	*Dave Robinson*	*Dave Valentine*
Eric Ashton	*Ernie Ashcroft*	*Frank Castle*	*Gerry Helme*	*John Warlow*
Lewis Jones	*Phil Jackson*	*Syd Hynes*	*Terry O'Grady*	*Kevin Ashcroft*

WIGAN
Timeless heroes

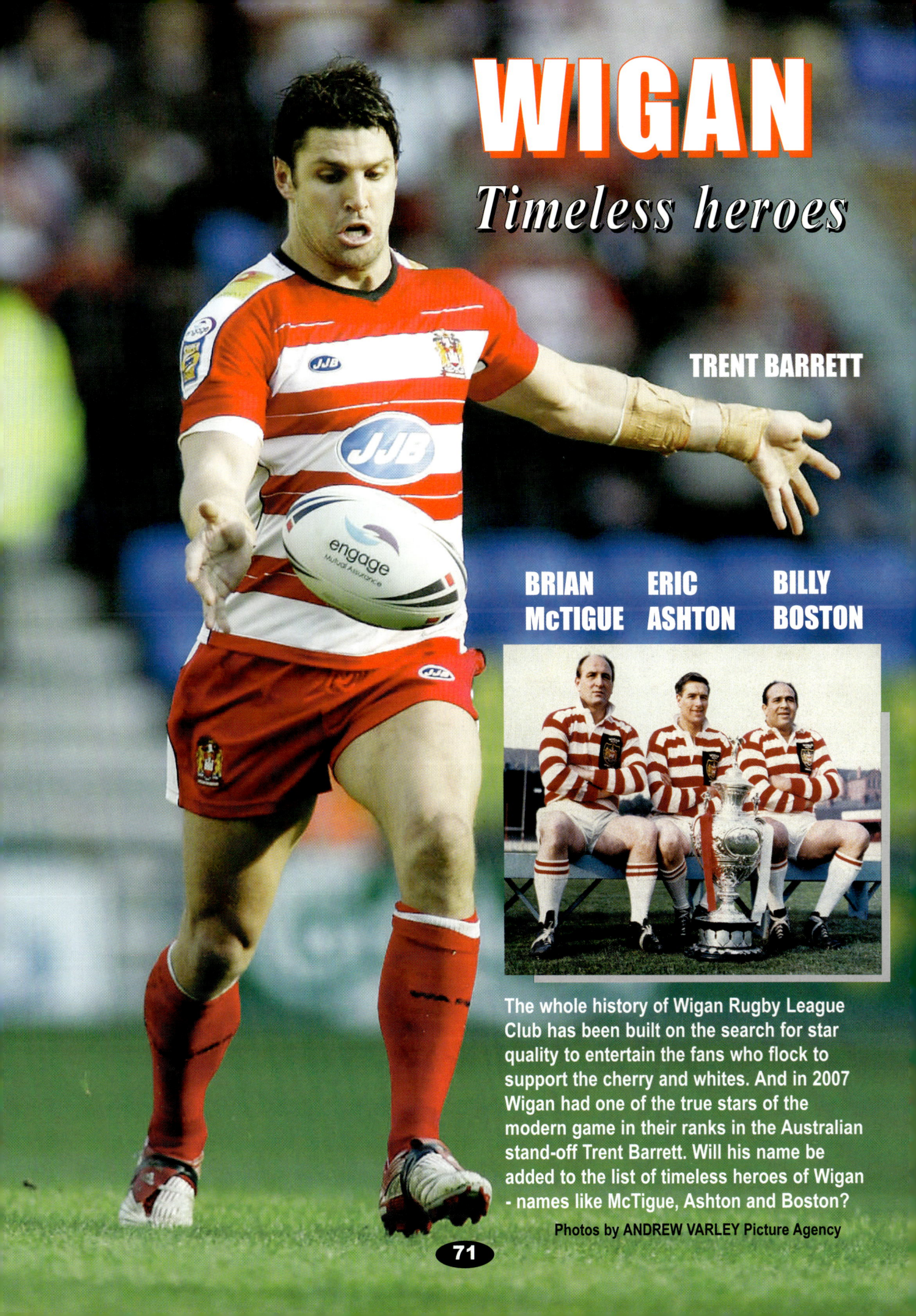

TRENT BARRETT

BRIAN McTIGUE **ERIC ASHTON** **BILLY BOSTON**

The whole history of Wigan Rugby League Club has been built on the search for star quality to entertain the fans who flock to support the cherry and whites. And in 2007 Wigan had one of the true stars of the modern game in their ranks in the Australian stand-off Trent Barrett. Will his name be added to the list of timeless heroes of Wigan - names like McTigue, Ashton and Boston?

Photos by ANDREW VARLEY Picture Agency

FAREWELL TO A ROLE MODEL FOR THE BRITISH GAME

SEEDS *of* SUCCESS

The National League season of 2007 saw the retirement of one of Cumbria's finest players - DAVID SEEDS

Photo by courtesy of MIKE McKENZIE

THE *Rugby League Journal* and our Annual you are reading at the moment is largely dedicated to paying tribute to the players of the past and to the nostalgia of keeping memories alive. But here we are paying a personal tribute to a player who has given so much to the modern game before calling full-time on an exemplary 14-year career at the end of the 2007 season.

(Above) DAVID SEEDS celebrates breaking the Whitehaven club's all-time try scoring reord in 2002; it was a record that had stood for over 40 years. *(Left)* On the attack in a memorable Challenge Cup tie against St.Helens in 2001.

A personal tribute by Rugby League Journal Editor - Harry Edgar

TWO of my favourite sportsmen, and two of Rugby League's outstanding players of the last decade, both hung up their boots as the 2007 season came to a close. One was Stacey Jones, a brilliant little footballer whose skills and contribution to the game have been recognised worldwide. The other was David Seeds, a quality player and person whose contribution to the game has been every bit as admirable as Stacey's, but whose recognition has been largely restricted to his home town of Whitehaven and among all the fellow professionals he played against.

I don't know Stacey Jones personally, I have only admired his footballing skills from afar like any Rugby League fan. But I do know David Seeds - I worked alongside him for the period I was involved as an official of the Whitehaven club, I helped edit his testimonial brochure and I have watched him closely as a fan throughout much of his 14 year career.

Many readers of *"Rugby League Journal"* outside Cumbria will not be familiar with David Seeds, but if they knew him and had watched him play over the past 14 years, they would share my admiration for him - because David has stood for everything that is good about Rugby League. Despite being surrounded by all the traits of the modern game, he has maintained all the same qualities that brought us to the game as youngsters many years ago.

Throughout those 14 years as a professional, I've never seen him commit a single foul or show any kind of dissent towards either match officials or opponents. He has always had time for his club's supporters, indeed no individual has typfied that bond between players and fans at a small-town club more strongly - on the day in 2002 when he broke the Whitehaven club all-time try scoring record in a match against Batley, after the game he bought a drink for every supporter in the club-house to celebrate.

Married with a family, David is very well qualified in his working life away from rugby and holds a responsible management job in local industry. As one who remains very dubious about the pitfalls of full-time professionalism in Rugby League, I saw him as a role model to spearhead the club's community work inspiring teenagers to understand they could work hard to achieve good qualifications and attain a professional career whilst at the same time playing top-class Rugby League.

On the field, David Seeds remained a specilaist centre - he always played centre - apart from a short, but mighty impressive, spell when switched to full-back by Kiwi coach Kevin Tamati. During that spell at full-back David scored the try he will single out as his most memorable in the grand total of 225 he scored to set a Whitehaven club record that is unlikely ever to be broken. That was a length of the field kick-return against Leigh one winter's day when the famous Seeds side-step worked to perfection.

Signed from local amateur club Kells, he was a BARLA international and played in the Amateurs' most successful ever youth team in Australia in 1993. He played a total of 357 games for Whitehaven, making him the third highest appearance maker in the club's history. Back in 1998, on its 50th anniversary, the Whitehaven club named its team of "Immortals" - and there's absolutely no doubt that, if that process were to be repeated in 2007, David Seeds would be included in the "Immortals" line-up.

You've got to laugh!

FUNNY STORIES FROM THE PAST IN THE WORLD OF RUGBY LEAGUE

Robinson's revenge!

Geoff Robinson bounds over for a try for Oldham against Liverpool City in 1960.

GEOFF Robinson was a mighty loose-forward who broke the Rugby League record transfer-fee for a forward when Oldham signed him from Whitehaven in 1959 to replace "Rocky" Turner in their pack.

As a young fellow Robinson had played Rugby Union for Workington Zebras but, after signing for the League team at Whitehaven, he got a first-hand view of the the old Rugby Union apartheid attitudes to those who changed codes - however, years later, Geoff got his revenge!

"I got my county cap for the full Cumberland & Westmorland Rugby Union side," recalled Geoff, "But I was warned not to play Rugby League and so my Union cap was presented to me through my mother's letter-box in a brown paper envelope. Not posted, somebody actually stuffed it through. The contrast when I got my Rugby League county cap was that it was presented to me in front of 8,000 people at Whitehaven. But I got my own back.

"When I'd finished playing League, I climbed quite extensively in Scotland, the Lake District and on expeditions to the Himalayas, but I got itchy feet so, although I was over 40, I started playing Union again with Aiden Breen, the ex-Huddersfield winger who I had played with in the same Cumberland Rugby League team. We turned out for Ashton Vandals, a motley crew of veterans at Ashton-under-Lyme, just for some fun. Aiden was a bit of a romantic, so he came up with the idea that we should play under the names of Weizmuller and Schwitzer. 'No one in the Rugby Union will recognise us with names like that,' said Aiden.

"But I got sent off in one game in Cheshire. The referee told me to get off the field and asked for my name. I said Schwitzer, and for some reason he didn't believe me. If he had asked for my first name, I *was* going to say Albert!"

Dewsbury's smart move

ON a murky day way back before the First World War, Dewsbury were playing Huddersfield in an important cup-tie at Crown Flatt, and Huddersfield were leading at half-time five points to three.

Dewsbury had stormed the Huddersfield line all the second-half - scrum after scrum had been fought out - yet they could not elude the fast Huddersfield spotters to score the vital try needed.

With one minute left to play, Huddersfield conceded a five yard scrum. Abe Evans, the Dewsbury loose-forward, and Neary, the scrum-half, held a hasty consultation and then Evans bent down as if to fasten a bootlace. Instead, he loosened it.

The pack got down and Dewsbury's hooker heeled the ball out. Evans held out a leg, Neary snatched the boot off and flung it to Milner. The uncertain light, the speed of the pass, and the manner in which Milner tucked the boot under his arm, deceived the Fartowners and half the side flung themselves on him.

Neary, meanwhile, picked up the ball which lay at the back of the scrum and walked over via the blind side. The referee awarded a try which was converted and Dewsbury won a memorable game.

Eddie got the bird!

EDDIE Waring, Dewsbury born famous BBC television commentator and newspaper writer, was the best known name in Rugby League for many years. During the 1960s era of "Classy Cas" Eddie would always refer to Castleford scrum-half Keith Hepworth as the "pigeon fancier." But, on this occasion, when Eddie put on a testimonial show, he was introduced to an unexpected guest by Heppy - and left holding the bird!

How Doug Laughton talked turkey

DOUG Laughton was one of the best recruits Widnes ever made - but the international loose-forward only got to join his hometown club from Wigan after an incident which is still remembered as the infamous *"Turkey Dinner Episode."*

It happened one day on the way home from a match in Yorkshire, as the Wigan team always stopped at the same hotel for a meal. And the players were always given the same standard dish - mixed grill - whilst the Chairman of the club had to have something special. On this particular Saturday, the Chairman was having a turkey dinner, but Duggie, who had got fed up of mixed grills, craftily intercepted the Chairman's plate from the waiter and tucked into the turkey. When the Chairman discovered his meal had gone missing he demanded, in a loud and angry voice, to know just who had got his turkey dinner.

When Doug owned up with a smile, the Chairman was so furious that he immediately shouted across the table: "Right, Laughton! You're going on the transfer-list tomorrow." And he did, to be quickly snapped up by Widnes.

DOUG LAUGHTON - tucked into the turkey!

Nuclear-powered vodka!

The sponsors' messages suggested they had come up with a recipe for nuclear-powered vodka - and Warrington's international winger Des Drummond and Whitehaven forward Geoff Simpson certainly had a good laugh about it. Friendly moments before kick-off in an "A" team match back in the late 1980s.

Keeping fit ... *Pipette style*

THE world of rugby has never known a more casual genius that the old French full-back Puig-Aubert. He was nicknamed *"Pipette"* because it literally meant "little chimney" - a tag he picked up as a teenager when he first started smoking two packets of strong cigarettes a day. He became a sensation on France's incredible first tour to Australia in 1951, with his casual approach to training, his enormous appetite and his love of wine and cigarettes. On the tour French players shocked Sydney folk by shooting ducks with catapults in a park and taking them back to their hotel to cook. Puig-Aubert turned down huge offers to play for St.George in Sydney because he said he would miss his *Gauloises* and *pastis* too much. Team-mates in France reckoned he sometimes took a pack of cigarettes on the field with him and would light one up if play was stuck at the other end of the field.

PUIG-AUBERT

Nobody home for forgotten Wires!

NO doubt when the most recent Challenge Cup finalists - St.Helens and the Catalan Dragons - returned from their exploits at Wembley in 2007, they were both treated to a lavish welcome home *(writes Garry Clarke.)*

However, 100 years ago, the Cup winners Warrington were not quite so lucky. When the victorious Wires team returned home from the Final they found they had been forgotten. Having defeated Batley, Hull, Huddersfield and Swinton to reach the Challenge Cup Final, Warrington faced Oldham at Broughton Rangers' Wheaters Field ground. A 17-3 victory saw Warrington lift the Cup for the second time in front of a crowd of 18,500.

The joyous Warrington team got on the train home and thousands of townsfolk crowded the station to meet their conquering heroes. A band played the team all the way to the Town Hall where a civic reception was expected. But, when they got to the gates, they were locked and all was deserted. Somebody had forgotten the local heroes!

CARTOON TIME

HULL KINGSTON ROVERS' RECORD SEASON 1966-67

"NO WONDER OUR ROBIN FEELS 'AS PROUD AS A PEACOCK'"

WHAT A STUPENDOUS EFFORT ALL THE LADS HAVE MADE TO MAKE THIS THEIR GREATEST SEASON EVER — FINISHING IN THE HIGHEST POSITION FOR OVER 40 YEARS

ABLY LED BY SKIPPER FRANK FOSTER

ASSISTED BY THAT WHIRLWIND ACE SCORER OF TRIES CHRIS YOUNG WITH A TOTAL OF 34 IN LEAGUE GAMES — A PERSONAL RECORD

RECORDS — ROVERS HAVE BEEN BEATEN ONLY SIX TIMES IN LEAGUE GAMES (ALL AWAY FROM HOME) AND HAVE SCORED MORE TRIES (178) — MORE GOALS (177) AND MORE POINTS (888) THAN IN ANY PREVIOUS SEASON

— AIDED AND ABETTED BY CYRIL KELLETT WHO BROKE HIS CLUB RECORD WITH A TOTAL OF 145 GOALS

FLASH FLANAGAN ONE OF THE GREATEST HOOKERS IN THE GAME — AND HE'S NEVER BEEN KNOWN TO CHEW THE "LUGS" OFF HIS 'OPPOSITE NUMBER'!

FRANK FOX (PERHAPS THE ONLY ONE THAT RUNS WITH A "PACK") — AND WEARS HIS "BRUSH" ON HIS CHIN

— AND HERE COMES THE GALLOPING MAJOR!

ALAN BURWELL A RIGHT GOOD CENTRE AND RUNS LIKE GREASED LIGHTNING!

BRIAN TYSON HE WEARS A "SAFETY BELT" — BUT SELDOM COMES OFF WORST IN A COLLISION

"HAPPY" HOLLIDAY A REAL GRAFTER

ROGER (THE DODGER) MILLWARD ALWAYS APPEARS TO BE IN DANGER OF GETTING TRODDEN ON — BUT CAN HE SCORE TRIES!

JOHN MOORE A REAL "TRY-ER"

DAVE ELLIOTT HE'S GOT A SAFE PAIR OF HANDS — AND A SWIFT PAIR OF FEET

MIKE BLACKMORE A DANGEROUS WINGER

— AND THIS LAD DOESN'T WAIT TO HEAR HIS PURSUERS SAY "BYE-BYE BABY BUNTING" WHEN HE'S SPRINTING FOR THE LINE

FINALLY — COACH COLIN HUTTON A GREAT JUDGE WHO SITS ON THE BENCH — BUT NEVER WEARS A WIG!

ERN SHAW 76

DON'T PANIC! THAT'S NOT THE DATE — IT'S HIS AGE!

The cartoonist's art by one of the best "Ern Shaw" - celebrating Hull Kingston Rovers success in the 1966-67 season. "Ern Shaw" was one of the most talented and best loved cartoonists in Rugby League.

Step into the Rugby League

TIME TUNNEL

as we take you on a photographic journey down memory lane in the game we used to know . . .

Memories of the very first World Cup Final played at the Parc des Pinces in Paris in 1954. Great Britain centre Alistair Naughton is the man with the ball as French winger Raymond Contrastin eyes up his opposite number Mick Sullivan. Great Britain won the Final, 16-12.

Super snap at Knowsley Road

A close up of this shot won a sports picture of the year award in 1958, but not many have seen the full wide angle view of this superb photograph showing St.Helens forward Walter Delves diving over for a try in a league match against Featherstone Rovers at a packed Knowsley Road. The famous referee Eric Clay *(on the right)* is well up with the play.

World's greatest try scorer ... finished with a kick

The great Brian Bevan scored a world record 796 tries in his Rugby League career - but his last act before leaving Warrington was to try a kick for goal in his farewell match against Leigh at Wilderspool in 1962. Bev's kick went very close . . . but it missed.

First French team to play at Wembley

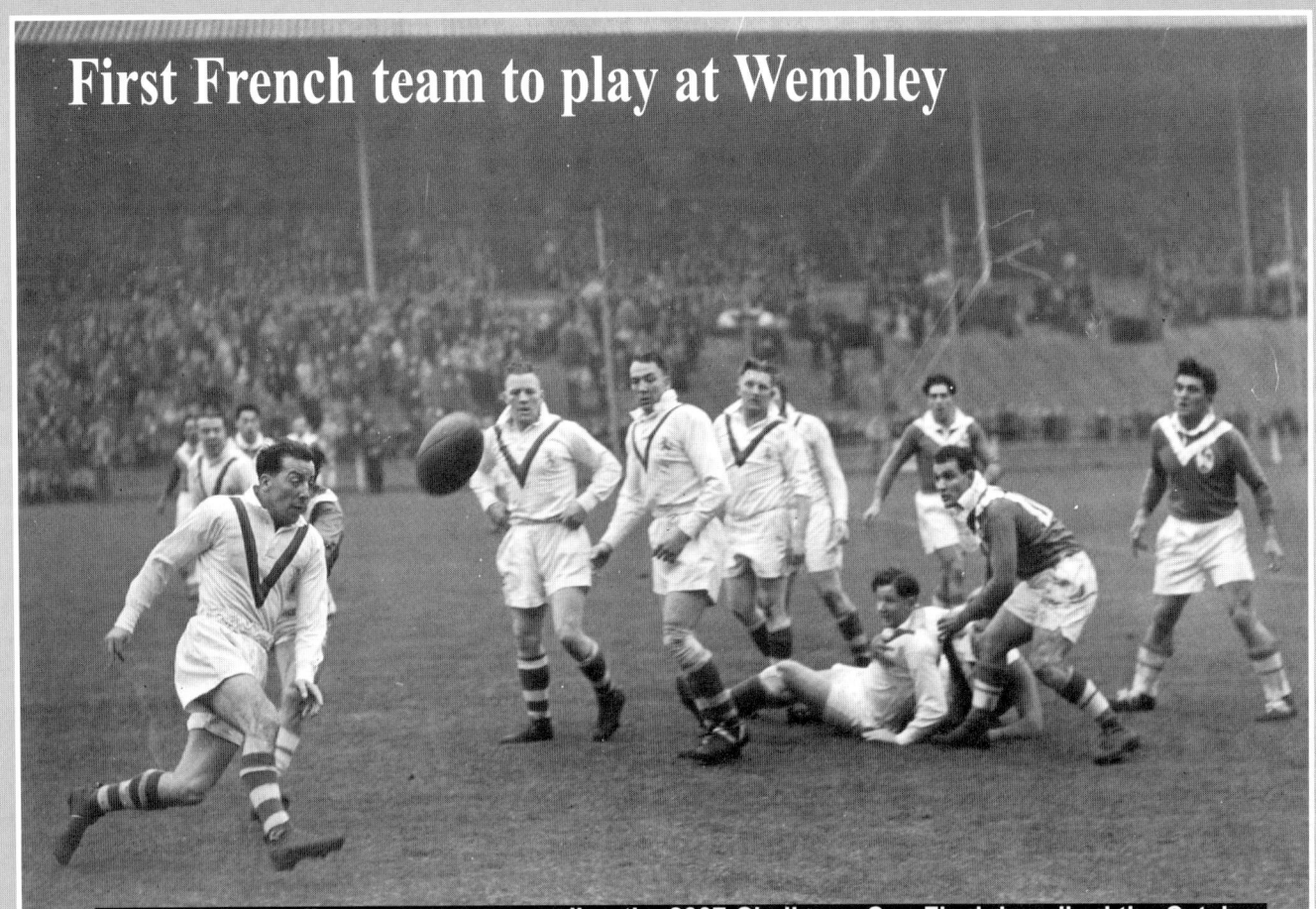

Much of the media coverage surrounding the 2007 Challenge Cup Final described the Catalan Dragons as the first French team ever to play at Wembley. Not true - in 1949 France played England at the Empire Stadium as this picture proves. Jack Fleming is the English player kicking ahead under the close watch of his forwards Jim Featherstone, George Curran, Bob Nicholson and Joe Egan (on the ground.) The French were delighted to win in London, 12-5.

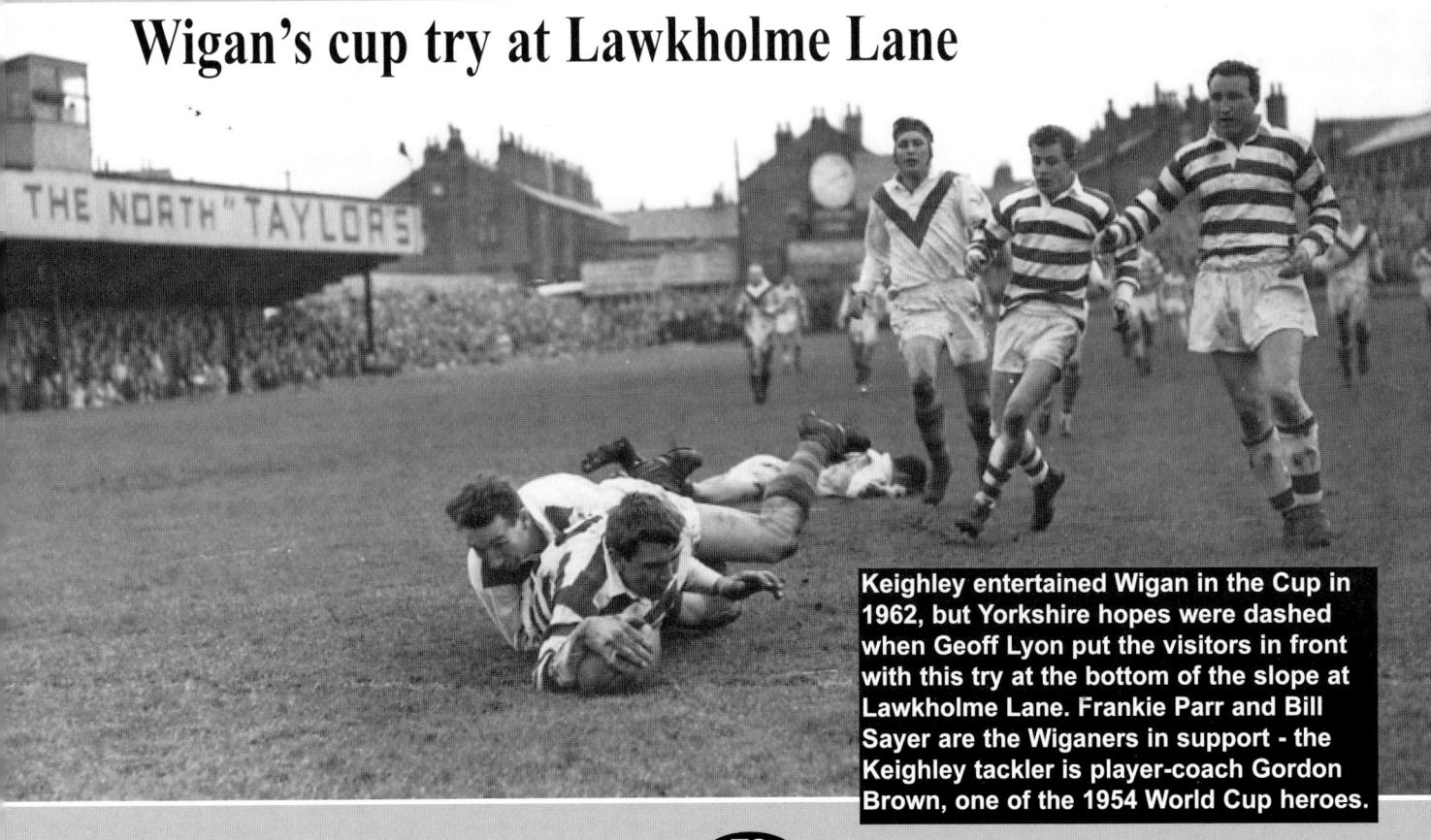

Wigan's cup try at Lawkholme Lane

Keighley entertained Wigan in the Cup in 1962, but Yorkshire hopes were dashed when Geoff Lyon put the visitors in front with this try at the bottom of the slope at Lawkholme Lane. Frankie Parr and Bill Sayer are the Wiganers in support - the Keighley tackler is player-coach Gordon Brown, one of the 1954 World Cup heroes.

Johnny's Boulevard boys

Hull versus Hull in the days when every club enjoyed pre-season trial matches. This was in August, 1968 and coach Johnny Whiteley prepares to watch his players battle it out for first team places.

The Rugby League Council

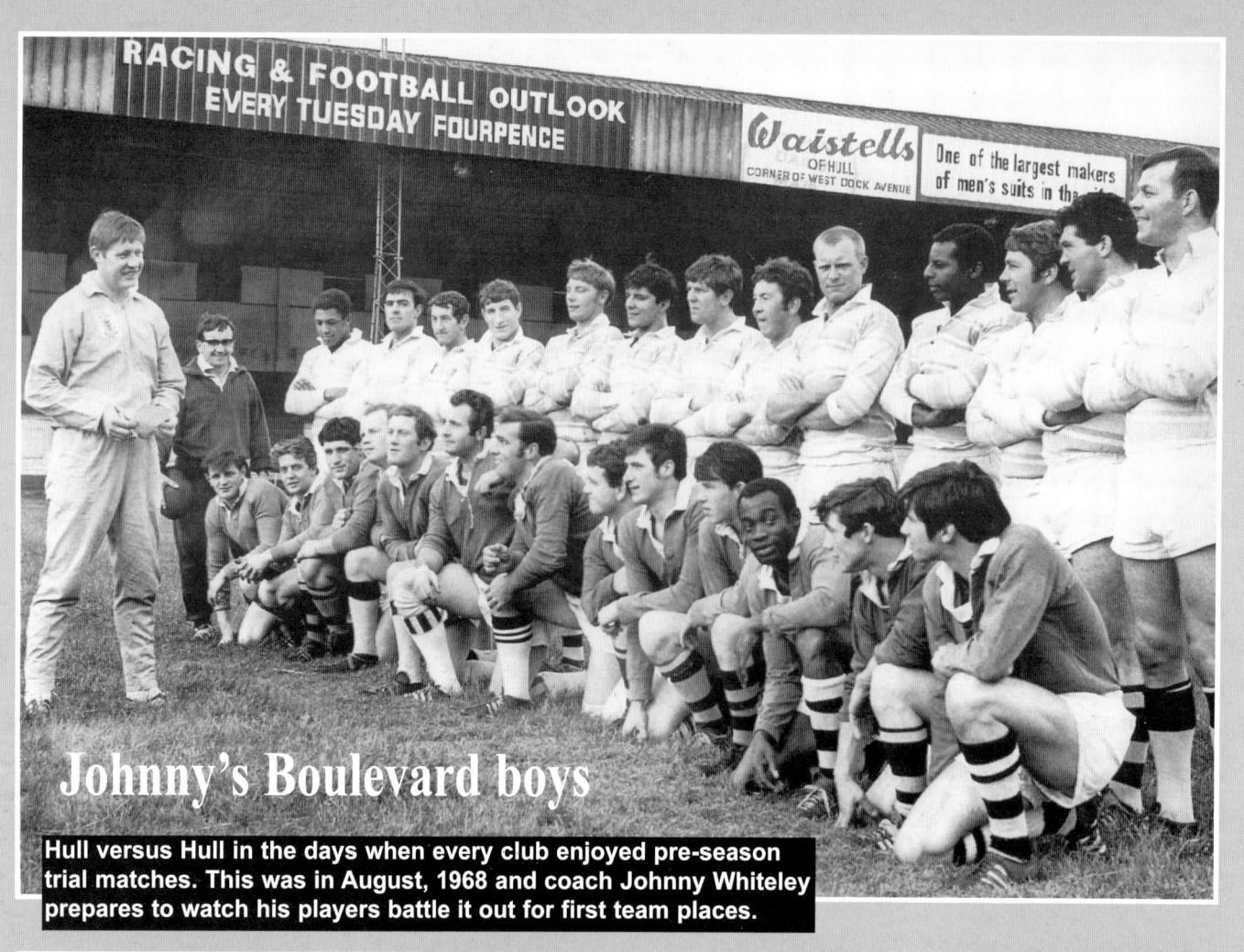

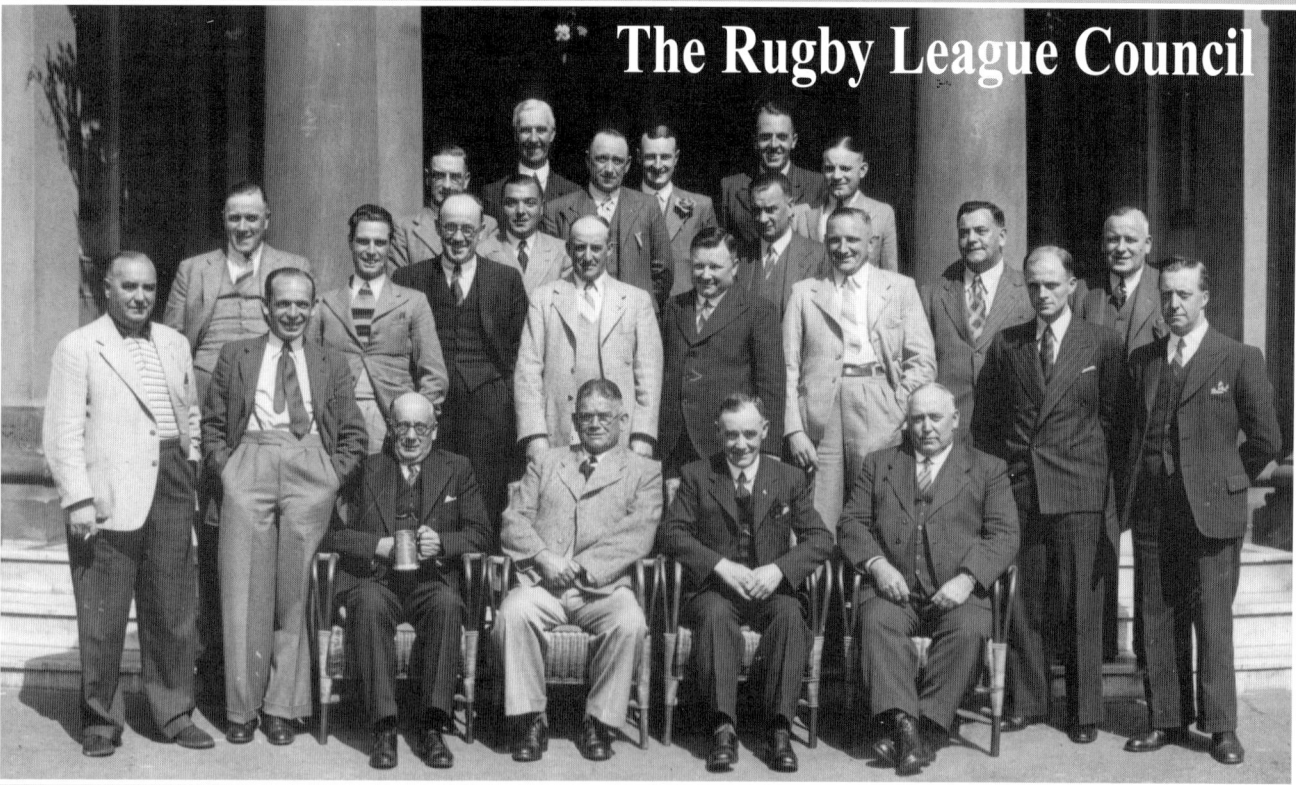

Members of the Rugby League Council - the game's governing body - pictured at one of their Annual General Meetings. The year would be either 1939 or one of the early Second World War years as Lance Todd, Salford's famous manager (who was killed in 1942) stands on the far left in the light jacket. The group includes two of the game's great publicists, Harry Sunderland and a young Eddie Waring.

Saints meet the 1963 Kangaroos

The excitement of a tour by the Kangaroos used to come around every four years - the first Australian team in living memory to go home with the Ashes was the 1963 side captained by Arthur Summons who did not play in a single Test match in England. The star, among many stars, of that tour was loose-forward Johnny Raper, pictured *(above)* about to touch down for a try in the Kangaroos' match against St.Helens at Knowsley Road. Kel Coslett is the Saints full-back on the right.

Oldham days at Watersheddings

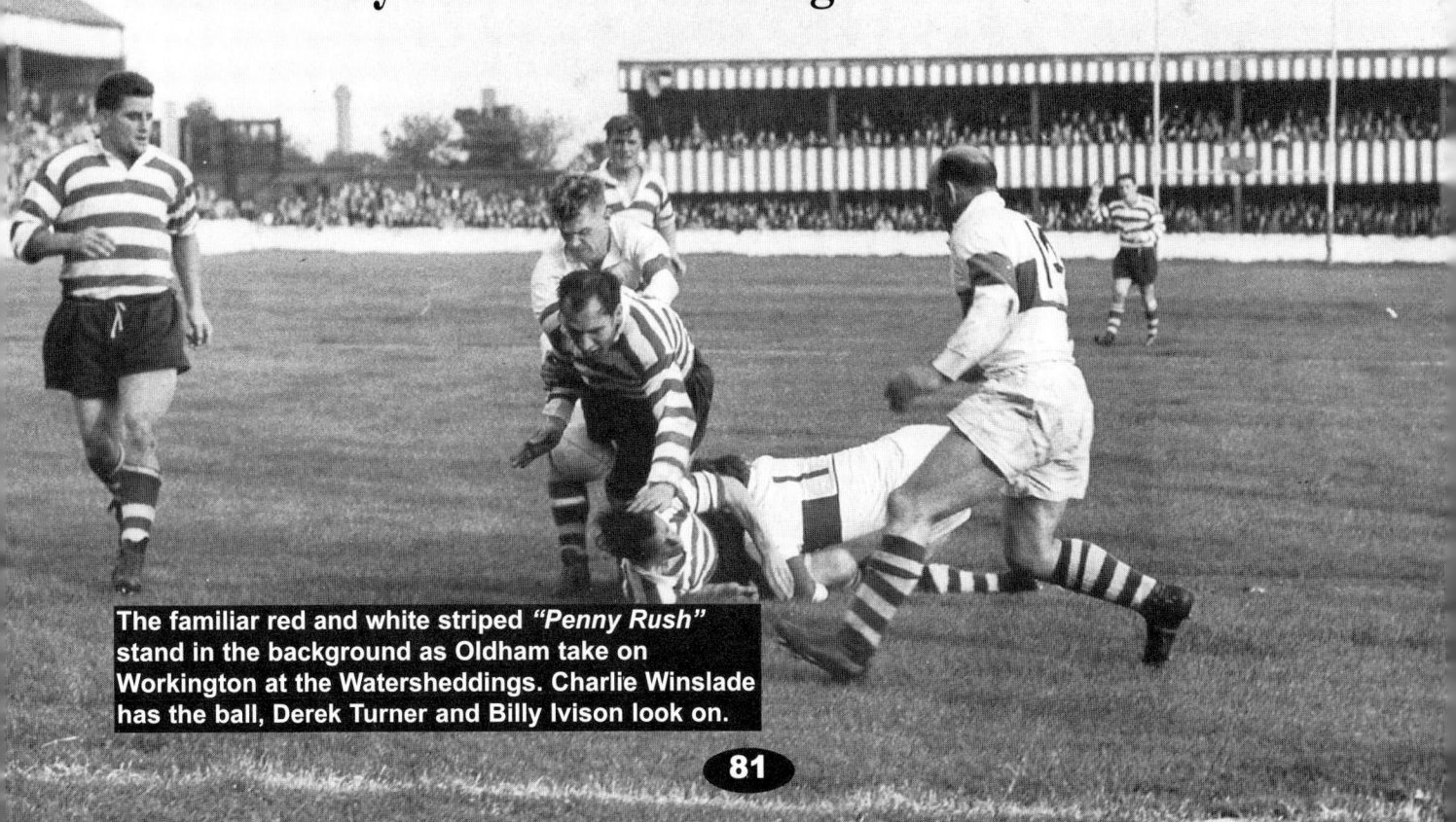

The familiar red and white striped *"Penny Rush"* stand in the background as Oldham take on Workington at the Watersheddings. Charlie Winslade has the ball, Derek Turner and Billy Ivison look on.

Wales at the Marseille Velodrome

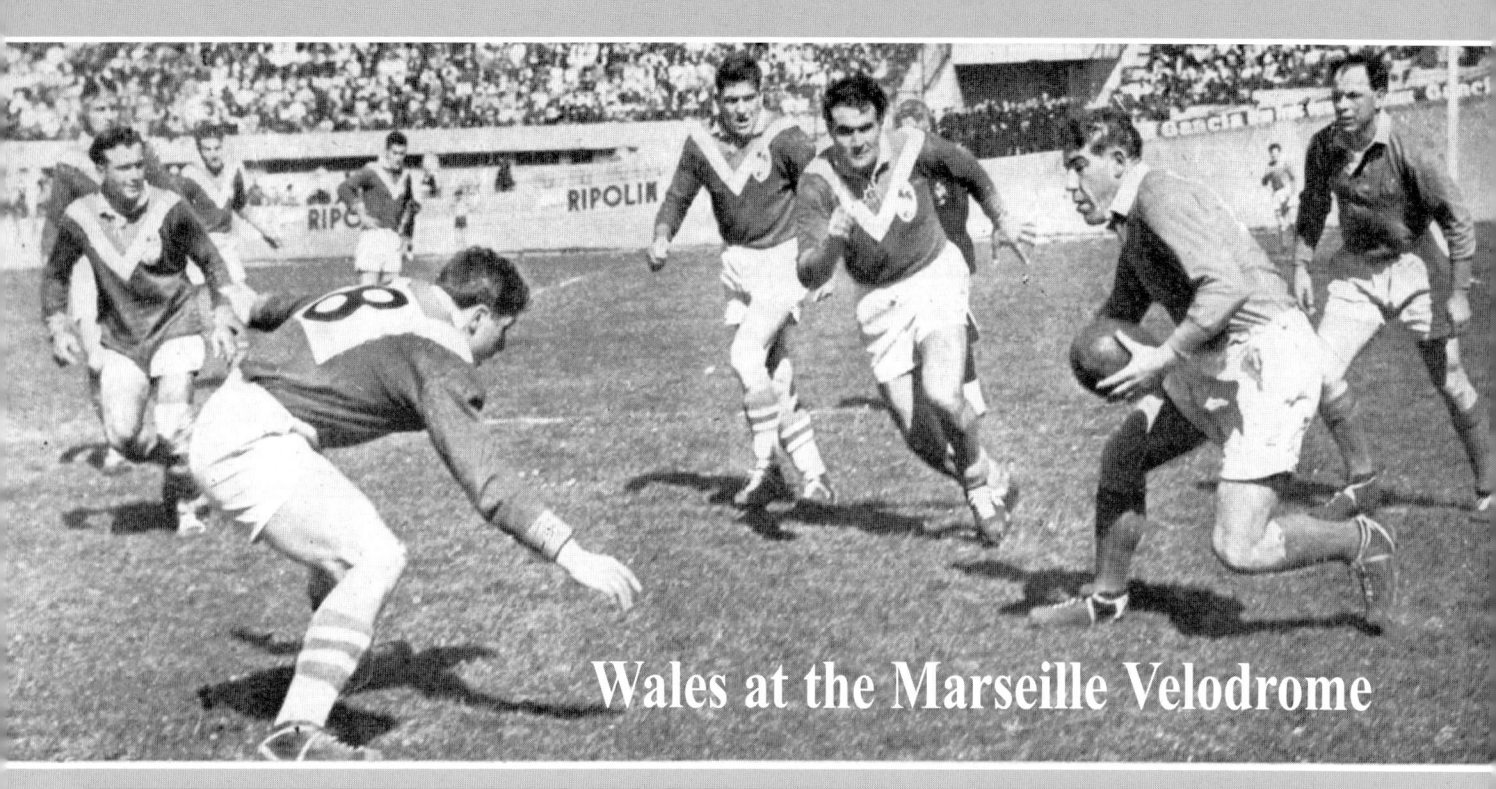

In the golden years of French Rugby League after World War Two, huge crowds would gather at the Marseille Velodrome stadium to watch the "Tricolours" play in the annual international championship. This picture shows Wales in action at Marseille in front of over 30,000 people in 1951, with St.Helens' forward George Parsons the man with the ball, being faced by the French prop Francois Rinaldi.

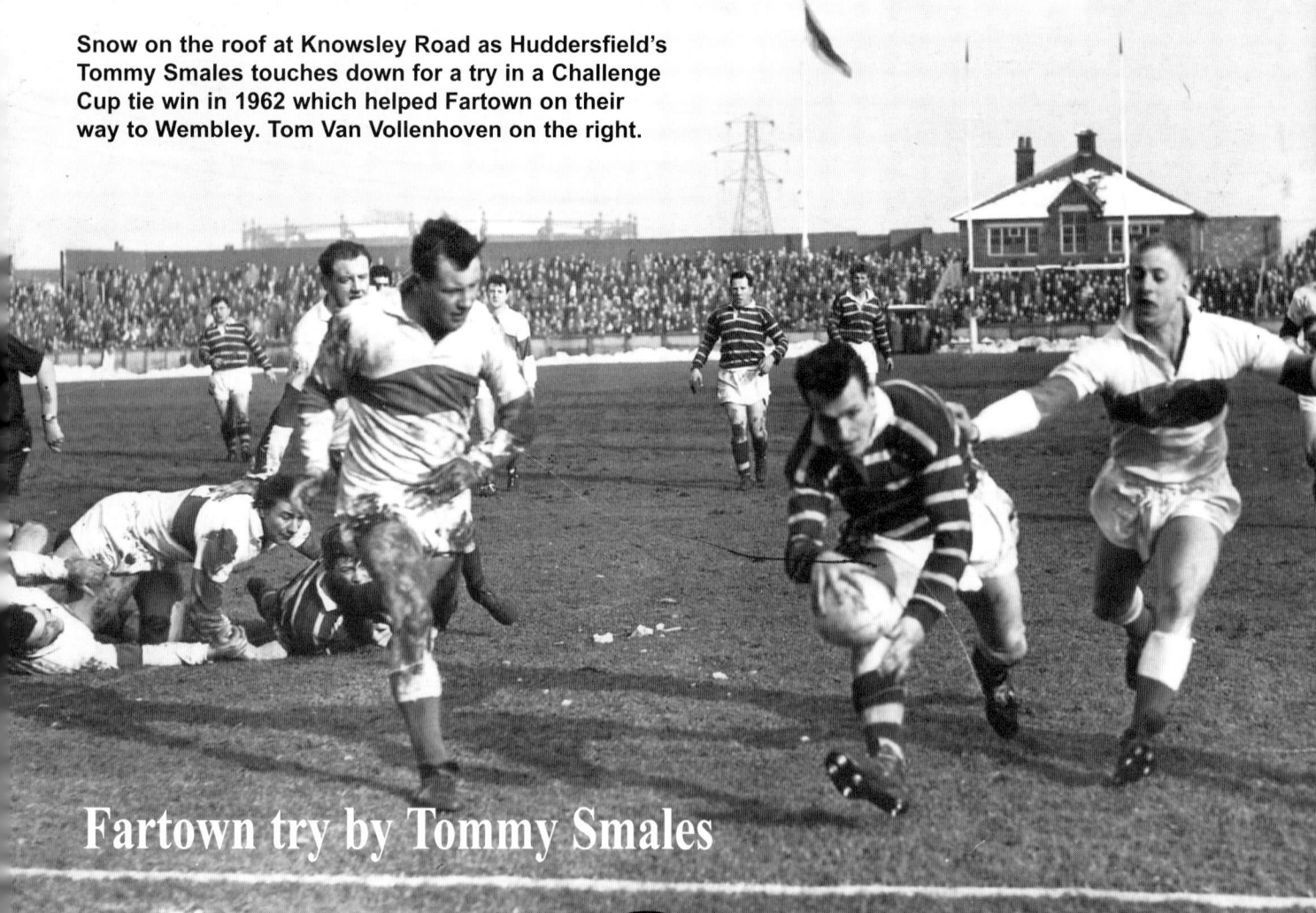

Snow on the roof at Knowsley Road as Huddersfield's Tommy Smales touches down for a try in a Challenge Cup tie win in 1962 which helped Fartown on their way to Wembley. Tom Van Vollenhoven on the right.

Fartown try by Tommy Smales

Bevan's magic

A typical illustration of how Brian Bevan could break a team's heart with a try out of nothing. In this match at Whitehaven in 1960-61, Bevan had kicked ahead and raced the full length of the field to score. Phil Kitchin leads the other 25 players on the field in pursuit.

Castleford at Wembley

Johnny Ward on the run as Salford's hooker Martin Dickens moves in when Castleford met the Red Devils at Wembley in 1969. In a tight encounter "Classy Cas" prevailed to win the Challenge Cup. Alan Hardisty and Mick Redfearn support.

83

Wigan entertain Leeds

Wigan versus Leeds has always been a highlight of any Rugby League season and this match in the early 1960s shows the familiar sights of Central Park as Leeds scrum-half Colin Evans is tackled by Geoff Lyon. 1960 World Cup winner Brian Shaw looks on for Leeds.

York at Clarence Street

A favourite ground in Rugby League was Clarence Street, in the shadow of York Minster. Here, York winger Brian Smith scores a try at the Minster end of the ground in March 1959.

Station Road tension

The tension of Challenge Cup semi-finals drew packed crowds to famous venues like Swinton's Station Road. In 1959 Wigan beat Leigh 5-nil to go to Wembley and Mick Sullivan scored the only try, diving over with Leigh half-back Brian Fallon in hot pursuit.

Odsal Stadium semi

Even bigger crowds could squeeze into Bradford's Odsal Stadium and in the 1961 Challenge Cup semi-final the terraces were packed to see St.Helens beat Hull. Terry Hollindrake is the Hull winger being bundled into touch by Mick Sullivan and Alex Murphy.

The first World Cup

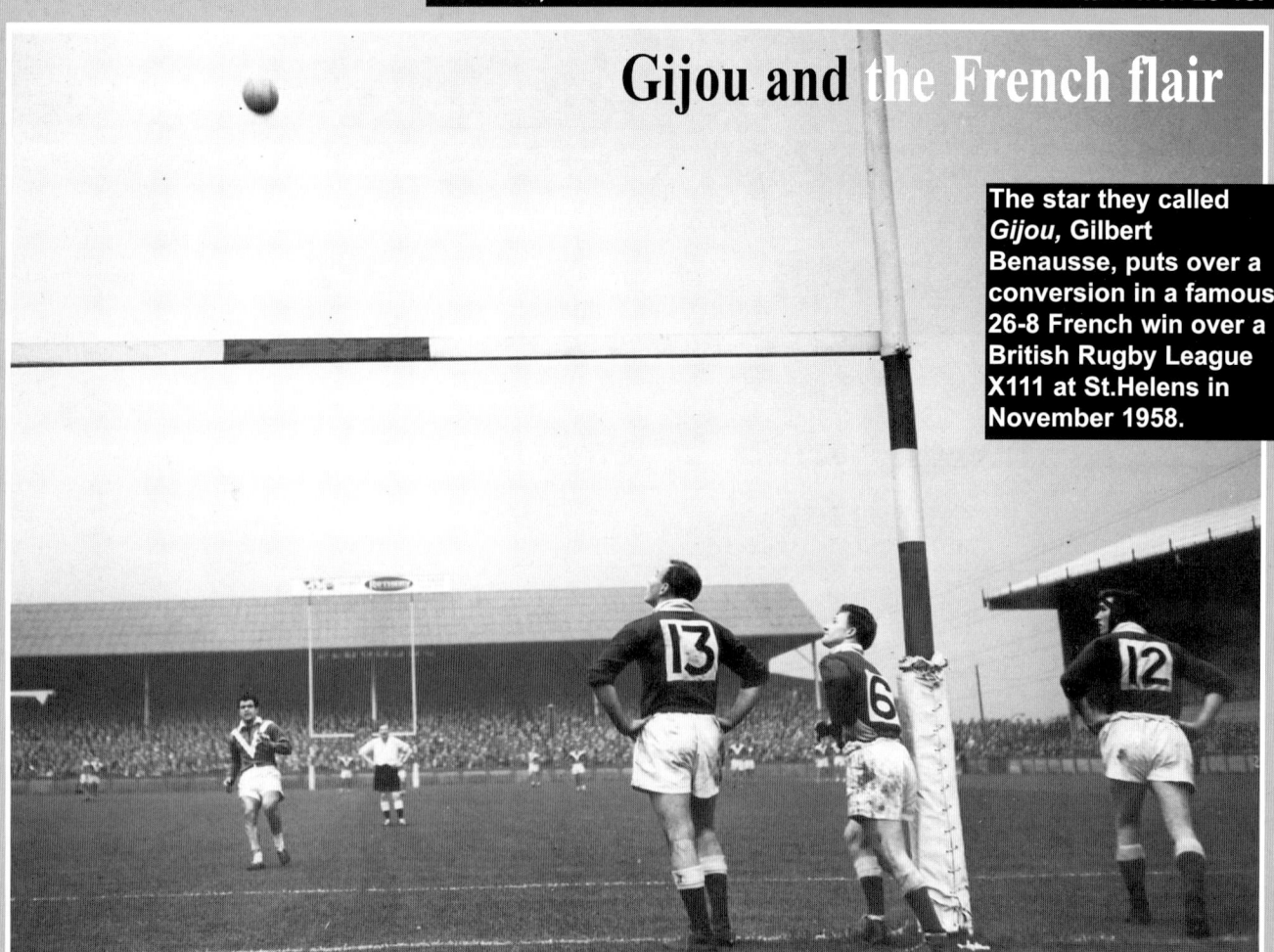

Great Britain's very first World Cup match was against Australia at the *Stade de Gerland* in Lyon, France, on 31st October, 1954. Robin Coverdale is the British number 10 in possession as skipper Dave Valentine, Basil Watts and Gordon Brown look on. Britain won 28-13.

Gijou and the French flair

The star they called *Gijou,* Gilbert Benausse, puts over a conversion in a famous 26-8 French win over a British Rugby League X111 at St.Helens in November 1958.

FOR FANS WHO DON'T WANT TO FORGET

GREAT STORIES, GREAT OLD PICTURES & GREAT MEMORIES

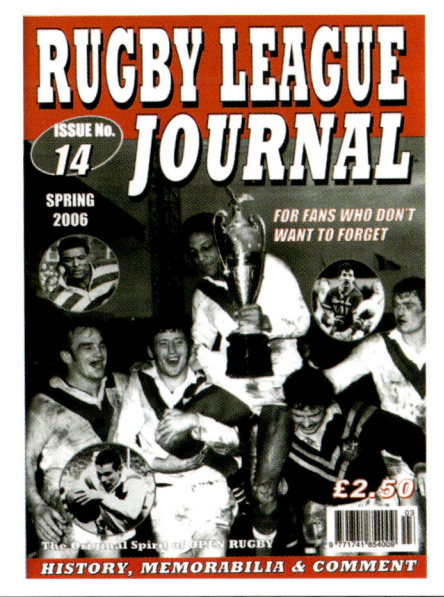

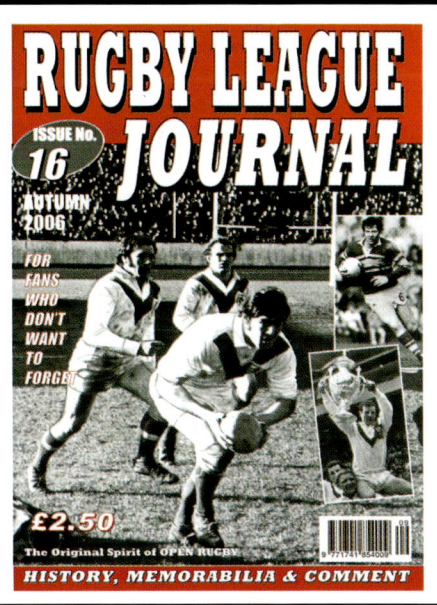

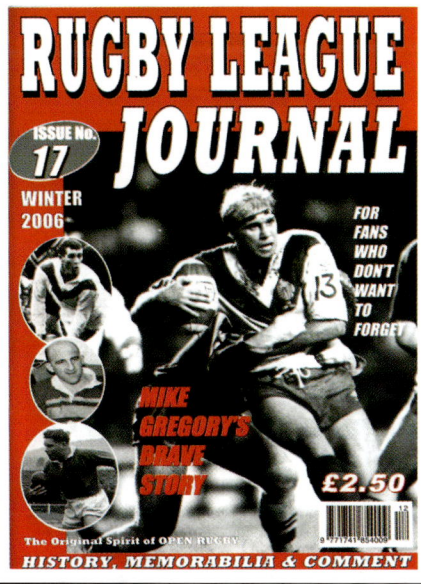

CATCH UP ON YOUR READING - BACK ISSUES AVAILABLE

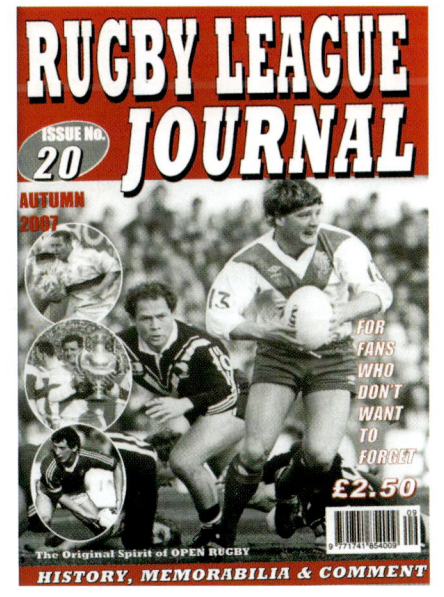

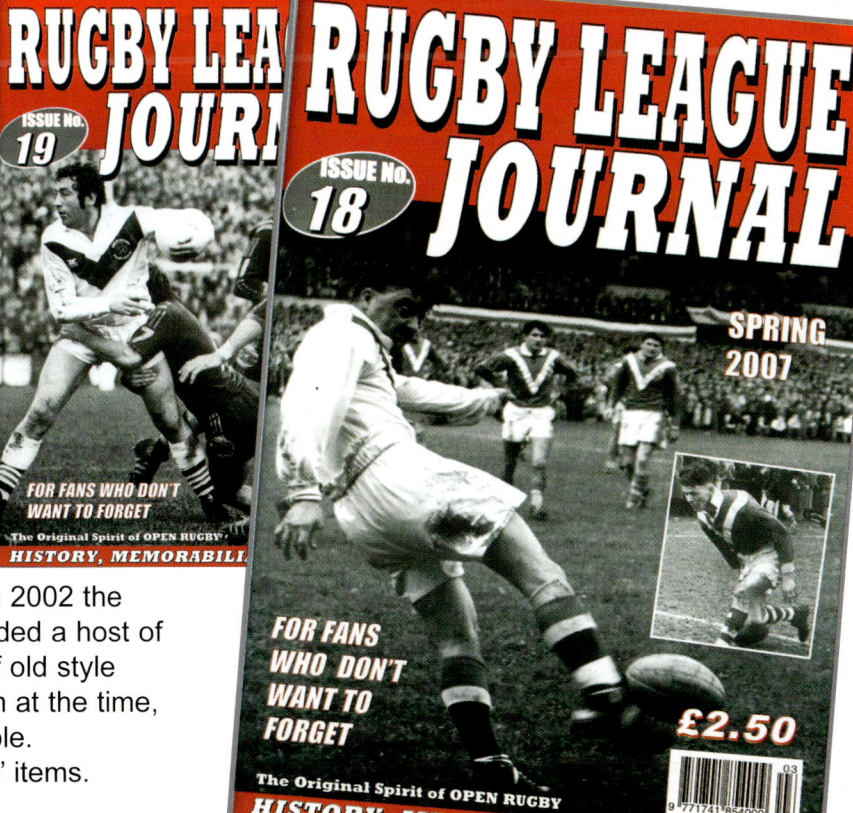

In the five years since its launch in 2002 the *"Rugby League Journal"* has provided a host of excellent reading and memories of old style Rugby League. If you missed them at the time, fifteen Back-Issues are still available. Don't miss these superb collectors' items.

ALL BACK-ISSUES PRICE £3.50 EACH *(incl. p&p.)*

There are fifteen Back Issues available, including all the issues pictured on this page. The issues available are: Numbers 1, 5, 8, 9, 10, 11, 12, 13, 14, 15, 16, 17, 18, 19 and 20. (Sorry, numbers 2, 3, 4, 6 and 7 are now sold out.) To order Back issues at £3.50 each, send cheque/P.O. *(payable to 'Rugby League Journal')* to: Rugby League Journal, P.O.Box 22, Egremont, Cumbria, CA23 3WA
E-mail: rugbyleague.journal@virgin.net   See our website at: www.rugbyleaguejournal.net

87

WORLD RUGBY LEAGUE'S NEXT NEW THING

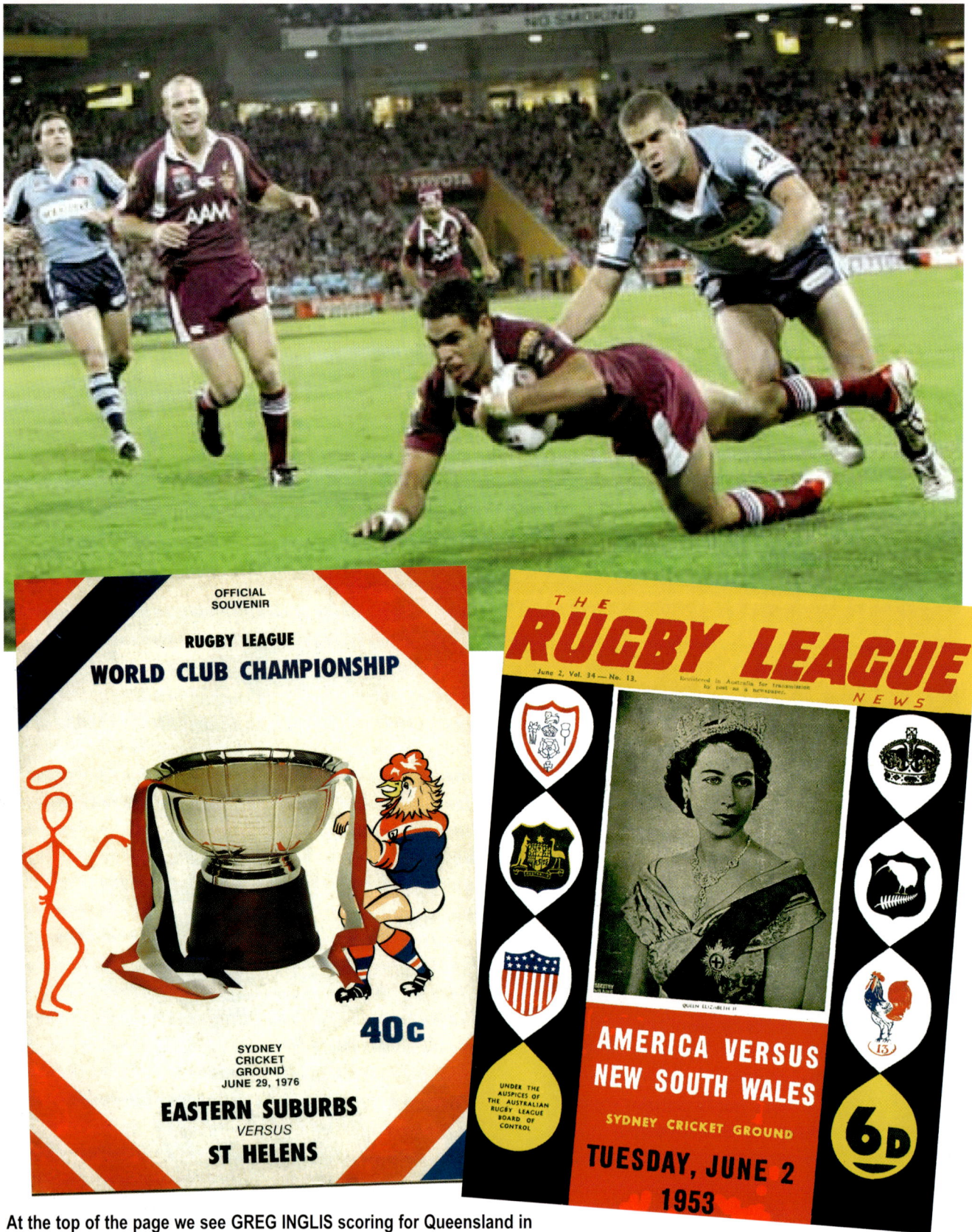

At the top of the page we see GREG INGLIS scoring for Queensland in the 2007 State of Origin series - Inglis is the young man set to be recognised as the next super talent of the world game, following in the recent footsteps of stars like Brad Fittler, Andrew Johns and Darren Lockyer. And the two programmes illustrated provide a reminder of Rugby League's search for new and exciting innovations in years gone by.
(Left) the first ever World Club Challenge match played between St.Helens and Easts at the Sydney Cricket Ground in 1976.
(Right) when the Americans first entered Rugby League as the "All Stars" toured Australia in 1953, this match versus New South Wales state. Hopes were high that the Americans could play in the inaugral World Cup in 1954, but it didn't happen.

SEE RUGBY LEAGUE HISTORY COME ALIVE
On DVD and Video

Including the 1965 classic Cup Final Hunslet v Wigan at Wembley

(Pictured) Hunslet's Alan Preece is tackled by Wigan's Laurie Gilfedder and Tony Stephens in the famous 1965 Challenge Cup Final. See it now on DVD.

Your chance to see again some historic Rugby League events. A large selection of DVDs and Videos now available which bring to life some of the great moments in Rugby League history. Including famous Test matches, Ashes battles and Wembley Cup Finals, plus historical documentaries.

Challenge Cup Finals include: 1962, 1963, 1965, 1967, 1968, 1969, 1970, 1971, 1972, 1973, 1978, 1979, 1982, 1985 and 1986. All available on both **DVD price £17.95 (plus £1.50 p&p)** and **Video price £16.95 (plus £2 p&p).**

To receive a free illustrated catalogue listing all titles available, send a first class stamp to: Open Rugby Nostalgia, P.O.Box 22, Egremont, Cumbria, CA23 3WA.

Open Rugby Nostagia, P.O.Box 22, Egremont, Cumbria, CA23 3WA
Or contact us by e-mail at: openrugby.nostalgia@virgin.net

To view more details - or order on-line via secure payment - see our website:
www.openrugbynostalgia.com

2007 - the year in Australia

The National Rugby League in Australia introduced a new club in the 2007 season - the Gold Coast Titans - who brought the former Kangaroos international star Mat Rogers back from Rugby Union and saw skipper Scott Prince *(above)* welcome him.

BOOM times, both at the gate and in the media continued for Rugby League in Australia throughout 2007 in a year that was best illustrated by the arrival of an exiting new club in the N.R.L. - the Gold Coast Titans.

The Titans further catered for the spiralling interest in the game in the sunshine state of Queensland, where Brisbane Broncos crowds have got back to pre-Super League levels and the North Queensland Cowboys continue to go from strength to strength going within just one game of achieving another Grand Final appearance and, once again, providing the competition's player-of-the-year in the shape of *Dally M.* winner Jonathan Thurston.

Attendances in the weekly rounds of the league topped three million for the first time since the N.R.L. was formed and only the second time in the history of the code in Australia

Those healthy crowd figures had much to do with the re-emergence of traditional Sydney clubs Parramatta, Manly and, best of all, Souths, as major forces in the game. South Sydney were never far away from the media headlines thanks to their joint owner being the Hollywood star Russell Crowe, but the bunnies were able to back up all the hype by qualifying for the play-offs for the first time in 18 years. Parramatta's pulling power was shown when an incredible crowd of over 50,000 turned out for their play-off match against Canterbury and, after the Eels' victory in that, there was a genuine chance that the 2007 Grand Final would stir memories of those famous clashes of the past by being a Parramatta versus Manly showdown.

It proved not to be as Parramatta went down at the last hurdle in Melbourne against the exciting team who had been many people's tip to win the competition from day one and who duly came through to beat Manly 34-8 in the Grand Final in front of an 81,392 crowd at the Telstra Stadium in Sydney.

It was Manly's first Grand Final for ten years but for Melbourne Storm, beaten finalists in 2006, this year's Premiership title always appeared to be their destiny. Coached by Wayne Bennett's former assistant, Craig Bellamy, and captained by hooker Cameron Smith - who, at the end of the season was named as Australia's captain in the absence of the injured Darren Lockyer - Melbourne played razzle-dazzle football all the way.

The fact that they had two of the most brilliant runners in the game in their ranks in the shape of Billy Slater and Greg Inglis, made them always exciting to watch. Inglis won the Clive Churchill Medal as the man-of-the-match in the Grand Final win over Manly but for the brilliant Billy Slater, it was incredible that he did not win selection for either the Australian team or for Queensland. His full-back role in the 2007 State of Origin series was taken by that other mercurial runner, Matt Bowen - as the Maroons beat New South Wales 2-1 to retain their crown. Queensland wrapped things up by winning the opening match 25-18 before a record Suncorp Stadium (Lang Park!) crowd of 52,498 and then repeating the dose 10-6 on NSW's home turf in Sydney.

Darren Lockyer, who has said he will retire from international football after the 2008 World Cup, captained Queensland to victory, before his season was finished by a knee injury. His absence had much to do with Brisbane Broncos struggling to make the play-offs.

WHEN THE AUSSIES PAY A VISIT

(Above) If looks could kill - some icy stares exchanged between Australian prop Steve Roach and Great Britain scrum-half Andy Gregory in the epic Old Trafford Test in the 1990 Ashes series. British captain Ellery Hanley seems to be keeping his eye on Roach as Mal Meninga and Paul Dixon help to calm down their respective team-mates. Australia saved the series in this Test with an injury-time try by Meninga.

(Above) The so-called "Dad's Army" Test victory for Great Britain at Odsal Stadium in 1978 - Phil Lowe and Roger Millward are pictured getting to grips with Aussie forward Rod Reddy as Kangaroo captain Bobby Fulton looks on.
(Right) One of Great Britain's blackest days as the Aussies won the Ashes at Swinton in 1963, Kangaroo Peter Dimond tries to hand-off GB's Jim Measures.

2007 - the year in New Zealand

AS Rugby League celebrated its Centenary Anniversary in New Zealand in 2007, it began planning its future by turning to its past.

Some of the most popular figures in the successful Kiwi teams of the 1980s were appointed to important positions as a new wave swept through the organisation of the NZRL following the embarassments and recriminations surrounding events of the previous year - not least the infamous "grannygate" affair of Aussie Nathan Fien in the Kiwi team during the 2006 Tri-Nations tournament.

In came Graham Lowe to the position of "Director of Football" - his first formal role with the national body, the New Zealand Rugby League, for 21 years. The former Kiwi coach Lowe has been involved at the very top level of the game in both Australia and England (with Wigan) and has remained one of the game's highest profile commentators in New Zealand.

And two of the former players who were highly respected footballers in the Kiwi teams Lowe coached in the 1980s, Howie Tamati and Gary Kemble, also found themselves back involved at the top level with the national team. Taranaki-based Tamati (also a former Kiwi coach) became the convener of the Kiwi selectors, whilst Kemble was appointed the New Zealand coach in succession to Brian "Bluey" McClennan who left the role to take up the head coach's job for 2008 with the Leeds club in England.

The appointment of Kemble, now aged 51, was in keeping with the NZRL's policy that their Kiwi coach should actually be resident in New Zealand. He has not coached a club at full-time professional level but has, for some years, been involved with New Zealand national teams at various levels. As a player, "Crayfish" Kemble was a very talented full-back who first became known to British fans in the late 1970s when he guested with the New Hunslet club. He became an international when he toured Britain and France with the 1980 Kiwis, after which he was signed by Hull, where he proved to be a very popular figure at the Boulevard. He played in three Wembley Cup Finals and was outstanding in Hull's Challenge Cup win in the Elland Road replay of 1982.

Kemble's first major assignment with the Kiwis was to be the "All Golds" tour to Europe and he quickly learned the harsh realities of being New Zealand coach when numerous top players started dropping out long before the selectors even got a chance to pick them. The biggest losses were the two men regarded as New Zealand's most talented and creative young individuals, Sonny-Bill Williams and Benji Marshall. Losing them to injury was nothing new - during Brian McClennan's two year reign as Kiwi coach Williams had figured in only one of the 15 Tests played whilst Marshall had played in just two.

Yet, despite all this and the large number of players coming through the Australian system now eligible for Kiwi selection, New Zealand's biggest hurdle in the immediate future is going to be all about finding a worthy successor to Stacey Jones. With the "Little General" now definitely hanging up his boots after more farewell performances than Frank Sinatra over the past two years, the Kiwis have no experienced replacement. All New Zealand's good moments under McClennan as coach came when Stacey was wearing the number seven jersey - without him they learned that success was much harder to find.

GARY KEMBLE pictured over 23 years ago - in action as New Zealand's full-back at Carlaw Park in 1984, with fellow Hull F.C. favourite DANE O'HARA in support.

Another imminent change on the international front for New Zealand is the abandonment of the annual "Anzac" Test match against Australia. Played as a memorial to Anzac Day at the end of April, the fixture had found a permanent home in Australia because that enabled it to be such a money-maker for the New Zealand Rugby League far in excess of anything they could generate on home soil. But the Kiwis decided they were sick of copping big defeats by the Aussies in a Test played at that time of year because of the lack of preparation time afforded their team and its inability to get access to players based with English Super League clubs, and would, therefore, only play Tests after the end of the club season. So, the record books with show that in the last "Anzac" Test in 2007, New Zealand were beaten 30-6 by Australia in Brisbane, with prop Roy Asotasi captaining the Kiwis for the first time.

There are also changes ahead on the domestic front in New Zealand - the 2007 Bartercard Cup competition was the last, and was won for the fourth consecutive year by the Auckland Lions, who beat Harbour League 28-4 in the Final in Auckland on 10th September. It has long been Graham Lowe's belief that the game in New Zealand would benefit more from competitions involving genuine traditional clubs rather than the manufactured "mergers" of the Bartercard Cup - and puplic support suggests he is right. Next year, the game will go "back to the future."

PLAYING AGAINST THE KIWIS

New Zealand came to Great Britain in 2007 exactly 100 years on from their very first international tour. The century of friendly rivalry between the British and the Kiwis has provided so many wonderful moments in the game's history. *(Above)* Ellery Hanley dives over for a try at the Kirkstall Lane end of Headingley during the magnifcent first Test of the 1985 series. The Kiwis is the picture are Gary Prohm, Olsen Filipaina and James Leuluia (hidden by the goal-post.) *(Left)* At Headingley again, but back in 1961, as New Zealand forward Brian Lee powers ahead chased by Britain's Brian McTigue.

At Auckland's Carlaw Park in the 1970 Test series. *(Above)* Tony Fisher gets to grips with New Zealand prop Doug Gailey, as Bob Irving looks on. *(Left)* Scrum-half Keith Hepworth tries to block a kick by Kiwi hooker Colin O'Neil.

2007 - the year in France

FRENCH Rugby League supporters, at last, could have a spring in their step after the remarkable success of the Catalan Dragons in 2007 brought a long awaited boost for morale among *Treizistes*. In the second season of the full-time professional club from Perpignan playing in the Super League, the Catalans continued to build their profile and support in the Roussillon area - and their achievement in reaching the Final of the Challenge Cup and playing at Wembley exeeded all expectations.

Indeed, those loyal French followers of the game who have been so beleaguered for so many years, had to pinch themselves to make sure it was not a dream - to see a French club playing at Wembley before over 84,000 people - the biggest crowd ever, anywhere, for a game involving a French team *in either code of rugby.* Crowds of around 8,000 were the average for the Catalans in their home games at the newly refurbished *Stade Gilbert Brutus,* as the momentum continued to grow providing the profile for Rugby League in this area of France as a serious, professional sport - something which it had struggled to achieve for over two decades.

Already the positive spin-offs are emerging with four new clubs forming at amateur level in the *Languedoc-Roussillon* area and thus reversing the downward trend of clubs and players being lost to the game which has been the depressing pattern over recent years in France. To be more accurate those four new clubs were actually three old, but dormant, ones being revived (including the once mighty St. Esteve) plus a new one in the traditional Rugby Union stronghold of Beziers.

The hope is that this inspiration provided by the Catalan Dragons can spread beyond their own area to the rest of the Rugby League regions of France. The profile in Perpignan is higher than it has been for many years, but what of the rest in the domestic competition?

The year 2007 in the French Rugby League belonged to Pia, who won the "double" of Cup and Championship for the second successive season. Whilst that very rare achievement will see Pia in the record books as - on paper - one of the greatest club sides the French game has known, the truth is their dominance has been more a reflection on the weakness of the competition. Pia is a team from little more than a village of less than 5,000 inhabitants, and they can hardly draw a crowd of more than a couple of hundred people to watch their home games - yet they have dominated the French game for the past two seasons, beating vastly bigger towns and cities like Carcassonne and Toulouse to the major honours.

The secret of Pia's success is that they have three local authorities all pumping money into the club, the vast majority of which they spend every year on Australian players. That is hardly healthy for French Rugby League, but it keeps Pia winning the trophies.

On a more positive note, Pia also had in their ranks Maxime Greseque, probably the most outstanding French player of recent vintage. Just as in 2006, Greseque's footballing skill and vision were the keys to Pia retaining both the Championship and the Cup this year. First up, they won the Lord Derby Cup, beating Carcassonne 30-14 in the final played at the *Stade Albert Domec* in Carcassonne. The local side A.S.C. had their hopes dashed away in torrential rain as Pia swept to a 24-nil lead in the first half. It was a disappointing end to a season that had promised much for a Carcassonne club that still carries the "sleeping giants" tag of French Rugby League.

Pia completed the second half of their "double" at the end of May when they beat Lezignan 20-16 in the Championship Final at the *Stade Michel-Bendichou* in Colomiers - a place which is very much a satellite town on the outskirts

MAXIME GRESEQUE - with his Pia team in the 2007 French Championship Final against F.C.Lezignan at Colomiers.

of the grand city of Toulouse, and which does not have a Rugby League club. It does, however, have an excellent stadium which suits the needs of the French Rugby League Federation, and a crowd just short of 9,000 were present at the Championship Final to see the undoubted player-of-the-year, Maxime Greseque, lift the Max Rousie Shield for the second time in his career - that still leaves him some way behind his illustrious father, Ivan Greseque, who won six Championships in his career with *XIII Catalan.*

Going so close to the Championship was a big achievement for F.C.Lezignan, probably the best supported of any club in the French competition in 2007 and coming back after their financial problems of a couple of years ago. Those same money problems also hit both Limoux and Carcassonne in the aftermath to the 2007 season, but they survived and will be joined in the 2007-08 season by another of France's most famous old teams, Racing Club of Albi, promoted to the Elite Division and making a big attempt to re-establish themselves as a force. Going the other way were Villefranche, dropping out of the elite.

BACK to the BRUTUS

(Above) Not a seat to be had in the packed grandstand at the Gilbert Brutus stadium for this Test between France and Great Britain on 16th January, 1966. This picture shows the elegant style of CLAUDE MANTOULAN swerving his way through the British defence led by GEOFF SHELTON, CLIFF WATSON and NEIL FOX. France won 18-13 in a match refereed by Eric Clay and broadcast live to the U.K by BBC Television. John Chapman, who was a team-mate of Mantoulan with the X111 Catalan club, recalls how he sat next to Eddie Waring as he did his commentary from Perpignan that day. Note the boots Mantoulan is wearing, they were running shoes with the spikes removed and replaced by studs - aimed at increasing speed. Chapman had brought this innovation with him from New Zealand and, after Mantoulan adopted the idea, all the other backs followed.

BRITISH fans who followed their clubs in the Super League to watch them play away at the Catalan Dragons in 2007, will have been aquainted with one of the most famous arenas in the French game - the *Stade Gilbert Brutus* - as the Perpignan club, at last, moved back to its newly renovated home ground after 15 years away.

After a financial investment of over four million euros from local authorities, the stadium was ready for the Dragons in 2007 after they had spent their first season in the Super League playing at various other venues. With a capacity of 9,000 the new "Brutus" was officially opened at a cermemony on 7th February, 2007 attended by a crowd of over 1,500 people. Ten days later, the first game was played there as an attendance of 7,630 turned out in torrential rain to see the Catalans play Wigan. A try by Alex Chan after four minutes of that game meant the honour of scoring the first points at the new Gilbert Brutus Stadium went to the big New Zealander.

In some ways it ironic that this stadium regarded as "the temple" of Rugby League in Perpignan is actually named after a Rugby Union man. Gilbert Brutus, born in nearby Port Vendres in 1887, died a martyr in the *Castillet* in Perpignan in March, 1944, after being tortured by the Gestapo. Decorated with the "Legion of Honour" during the First World War, he had been a member of the secret army of the Resistance when he was captured in 1944.

Gilbert Brutus had been an outstanding player in Rugby Union, and also a coach, official, national selector and leading referee. He was also well known as a Politician in local government. The original stadium was named after him in September, 1944, but it was 1962 before a programme of renovation saw the newly developed Gilbert Brutus Stadium dedicated as the home of the 13-aside game in the city. The first Test match played there was a 23-13 win over Great Britain in March, 1962 in front of 12,500 spectators - and some 20 more big international games were to follow there between 1962 and 1992 when the ground was temporarily abandoned.

Amateur Rugby League in 2007

INTERNATIONAL tours were high on the agenda for Amateur Rugby League in 2007, with BARLA sending no less than four different age-group teams overseas to help the game in some of its development countries - all the tours being self-funded by the players and their clubs.

The BARLA Under-18s went to play in Serbia; the Under-21s to Russia; the Under-23s to Italy; and the Open-Age team to South Africa. All returned home with 100 per cent success records but, moreso, all played a big role in helping show the new nations what Rugby League is all about. The toughest tour was the one undertaken by the BARLA senior team in South Africa where they met very rugged and physically tough opposition in the two "Tests" - the British Amateurs won all four tour games, including those "Tests" against the South African Rhinos 30-12 and 42-10.

The British team were captained by forward Anthony Broadhead of Thornhill (Dewsbury) and their coaches were Chris Middlehurst and John Fieldhouse.

Meanwhile, the "other" British Amateur international team - the Great Britain Community Lions captained by Mel Alker of Wigan St.Patrick's - were defeated at home to France "B" in March, 33-20, in a match played at the home of the Mayfield Amateur club in Rochdale. Coached by Jimmy Taylor, this representative side which comes under the jurisdiction of the R.F.L.'s Community Board, have been told they can look forward to a programme of international events over the next couple of years which will involve not only the annual home and away fixtures with France "B," but also a trip to Australia to take part in a new series involving teams from Queensland and New South Wales.

Sadly for the BARLA representative teams and the many supporters in Lancashire, Yorkshire and Cumbria who look forward to seeing high-quality Amateur Rugby League fixtures, the tour by the Australian Aboriginals scheduled for Autumn 2007, had to be cancelled due to a lack of funding back home in Australia.

AT home on the domestic front, Skirlaugh emerged as the top Amateur club in the country following their 8-6 victory over Leigh Miners in the National Conference Premier Division Grand Final. Leigh Miners had finished top of the Division, but it was the powerful Skirlaugh side which stormed home in the play-off staged at Rochdale's Spotland stadium. The accolade of National Conference Champions was another feather in the cap of Skirlaugh, the village side from Humberside, following their earlier triumphs in the BARLA National Cup.

The strength of the amateur game in the city of Hull was emphasised with not only Skirlaugh finishing second on the league ladder, but also East Hull, West Hull and Hull Dockers achieving third, fourth and fifth positions respectively.

Skirlaugh's achievements in 2007 were capped in September when they travelled to France and won the "European Challenge Cup" by beating the French Division Two champions Bias by 28 points to 18.

The Amateur National Cup provided a real turn up for the books when Halton Simms Cross, from the North West Counties League, emerged ahead of all the top sides from the National Conference, to win the Tom Mitchell Trophy when they defeated Ince Rose Bridge 23-8 in the Final, staged in 2007 for the first time at Fylde Rugby Union Club. Simms Cross became the very first Widnes Amateur club to reach the BARLA National Cup Final, and their second-rower Shaun McDermott won the prestigious "Tom Keaveney Award" as man-of-the-match. Coach Rob Shone was later named as the coach-of-the-year in BARLA's end of season awards.

Other BARLA award winners in 2007 were: Jimmy Rogers of Saddleworth Rangers as the Open-Age player-of-the-year and Chris Forster of Rylands (Warrington) as the Youth player-of-the-year.

Yorkshire maintained the Amateur County Championship for a third successive year, beating both Lancashire and Cumbria; whilst Siddal were champions in the Amateurs' prestigious National Youth League (sponsored by Halifax Home Insurance), beating West Hull in the Final at Headingley. In the first full Women's international between the two nations, England beat France 16-2 in July at Lescure, near Albi. The victorious English girls were captained by experienced centre Natalie Gilmour.

The BARLA Great Britain Under-18s on their promotional tour to Serbia in 2007.

Memories of the Great Britain Amateur international team - this is the BARLA touring team to the South Pacific in 1994, which was captained by John Brocklebank, one of the game's "corinthian" figures who stayed an amateur throughout his career.

BARLA maintained proud record of Amateur internationals

IT was highly appropriate that BARLA's prestigious Silver Boot Award in 2007, given for outstanding service to the Amateur game, went to Douglas Hird of Shaw Cross (Dewsbury) in a year which celebrated the 30th anniversary of the very first BARLA Youth tour to Australasia.

Mr.Hird was co-manager of that 1977 tour which has come to be acknowledged as such an important landmark for Amateur Rugby League in this country as it was the first time British Amateur players had been given the opportunity to travel beyond Europe. Just four years after the birth of the British Amateur Rugby League Association, their Under-18 tourists went to play in both Australia and New Zealand on a tour which included playing a curtain-raiser on the Sydney Cricket Ground before the 1977 World Cup Final between Australia and Great Britain.

A year later, in 1978, BARLA pushed back its frontiers even further when their first Great Britain Open-Age tour took them not just to Australia and New Zealand, but also to Papua New Guinea as they became the first sporting organisation to make an extensive tour to that largely unknown country where Rugby League is the national sport.

RUSSELL PEPPERELL of Seaton (Cumberland) pictured in his England Amateur international jersey before playing France at Bordeaux. He went on to captain Huddersfield the last time Fartown won the Challenge Cup at Wembley in 1953.

The Great Britain Amateur touring team in 1978 was captained by Bob Colgrave from Hull, who began a long line of BARLA captains who came to be recognised as some of the true "Corinthian" figures of British sport as all resisted opportunities to move into the professional ranks and stayed in the Amateur game - among them such excellent players and fine leaders as: Mick Appleyard (Leeds), Steve Critchenson (Hull) John Brocklebank (Egremont) Dave Roe (Hull) and Paul Davidson (Wath Brow.)

Since the pioneers of 1977, BARLA international teams have enjoyed many overseas tours to the southern hemisphere and to a variety of other nations across Europe, plus Morocco and the U.S.A. Before the birth of BARLA, Amateur Rugby League internationals were restricted to the annual match with France, which were played at home or away in alternate years, contrasting with the Junior international matches which began in 1947 with a 32-10 win by France over England at Warrington. The first Open-Age Amateur international was staged in April 1934, in Paris, where England won 23-9. England won again the following year at Halifax 16-8, before the French Amateurs got their first of eight consecutive victories over the English, in 1937 at Bordeaux, 12-2,

New Horizons in 2007

AS a participation sport at amateur level, Rugby League has never known such widespread activity as it continued to see develop in 2007 - both to new destinations across the British Isles and internationally.

Meanwhile, at professional level, the game's profile in South Wales enjoyed a marvellous boost with the success of the Bridgend based Celtic Crusaders in winning the National League Division Two title. Notwithstanding the fact that the Celtic team's strength was based largely on Australian players, the fact that Wales has a successful team being promoted to Division One and is talking optmisitically about establishing a Super League franchise in the Principality, presents an opportunity for the sport to win new followers.

Likewise in the south east of England where the London Skolars enjoyed their best season to date and saw their coach, the New Zealander Latham Tawhai, win the award as the National League Two coach-of-the-year.

At amateur level, the summertime Rugby League Conference continued to take the game to more parts of the England, plus to Wales, Scotland and Ireland. There was particularly pleasing progress in Devon, which was heartwarming for those enthusiasts aware of Rugby League's fascinating history in the soutn-west.

St.Albans emerged as the Rugby League Conference national champions, thus receiving the Harry Jepson trophy, after beating Coventry on their own ground in the Grand Final 28-20. It was a first ever trophy for the St.Albans club which enjoyed a remarkable upsurge in fortunes after ending their 2006 season in some disarray and with their very future in doubt. Like several other development area clubs, St.Albans found that the Rugby League's now defunct National League Three had brought them to their knees. Their survival could only be based on local development and a huge dose of reality, and their subsequent success in 2007 was a fitting reward for the efforts of club stalwarts like Gary Tetlow.

There was a similarly happy story in 2007 in the south west of England where the Bristol Sonics club came back to be the West Midlands Regional Champions, and strong come-backs from both the Coventry and South London clubs. Perhaps the highest profile club in the south of England were the Kent Ravens, and the Bedford Tigers enjoyed a successful campaign to finish as runner-up to the Widnes Saints in the Conference Regional Grand Final.

Further afield, Students continued to push back the boundaries for Rugby League development. At the elite level the Great Britain Students put in a great effort when hosting the Australian Universities during July before going down very narrowly in a three-match "Academic Ashes" series. With the series level, one Test apiece, the Aussies squeezed a 10-6 victory in the decider played at Wakefield. The British Students star had been winger Stuart Sanderson of Teeside University, an experienced player at the top level of Amateur Rugby League with the Wath Brow Hornets club. And the Great Britain Student Pioneers this year travelled to Latvia to help develop the game by playing in a three-way Nines tournament with the host nation and Estonia.

The greatest achievement came from the boys from Year 11 of the Whitehaven School who, fresh from their triumph as the Carnegie Champion School for 2007 in their age group, were invited to represent England in the European Nations Under-16 championships in Serbia. The Whitehaven boys, whose skills had all been perfected as members of local BARLA clubs like Kells, Hensingham and Wath Brow Hornets, hammered both Russia and Serbia and then caused a massive upset by beating the French national side 14-12. The RFL's publicity proudly procliamed England as European Champions, but little did the wider world realise that it was an individual schools team from Whitehaven who had achieved that. At home, the Champion Schools competitions continued to grow, in 2007 under the banner of the Carnegie sponsorship, and it was a particularly successful year for Castleford High Schools, winners in no less than four age groups.

(Above) **How the local newspaper in West Cumbria saw the triumph of the Whitehaven School team in the European Nations Under-16s tournament in Serbia during 2007.**

For many of those who have championed the expansion of Rugby League to other areas of the country, and particularly for the pioneers of the Conference, the continued trend in the RFL-backed summer compeititions of a concentration on Yorkshire clubs was perplexing. With their National League Three consigned to the dustbin, its replacement in 2007 - the Conference National League - was won by Featherstone Lions. Of the nine teams who completed the season, only the valiant Hemel Hempstead and Gateshead Storm came from areas of the country beyond the Yorkshire and old Lancashire boundaries.

Rob captained Harlequins and England ...

... but his greatest memory remains Cup glory with Egremont

Photo by ANDREW VARLEY Picture Agency

ROBERT Purdham has achieved plenty since he left working on his family farm near Gosforth in Cumbria to become a full-time professional player in London. He signed for the then London Broncos in December 2001 from Whitehaven where he was beginning to establish himself as a talented stand-off and won England Under-21 honours.

Since then, Robert appears to have doubled in size from a skinny young stand-off into a powerfully built second-rower, and in 2007 he remained the longest-serving player with Super League's club in the capital city. Now under the banner of the Harlequins, Purdham has been the club captain for the past two seasons and also captained England to victory in the 2006 Federation Shield competition.

But, despite the prestige of winning such honours, Robert still regards the biggest highlight of his footballing career as the night his amateur club, Egremont Rangers, beat the pros' of Workington Town 18-nil in the Challenge Cup in 1998. Playing alongside his elder brother Garry, the younger Purdham scored Egremont's opening try in that famous victory. The previous season he had also been a big part of Egremont being crowned BARLA National Conference champions and, like brother Garry, he was capped as a BARLA Youth international.

Those beginnings are a long way from Harlequins, but Robert Purdham is one of their's, and Rugby League's, finest ambassadors.

99

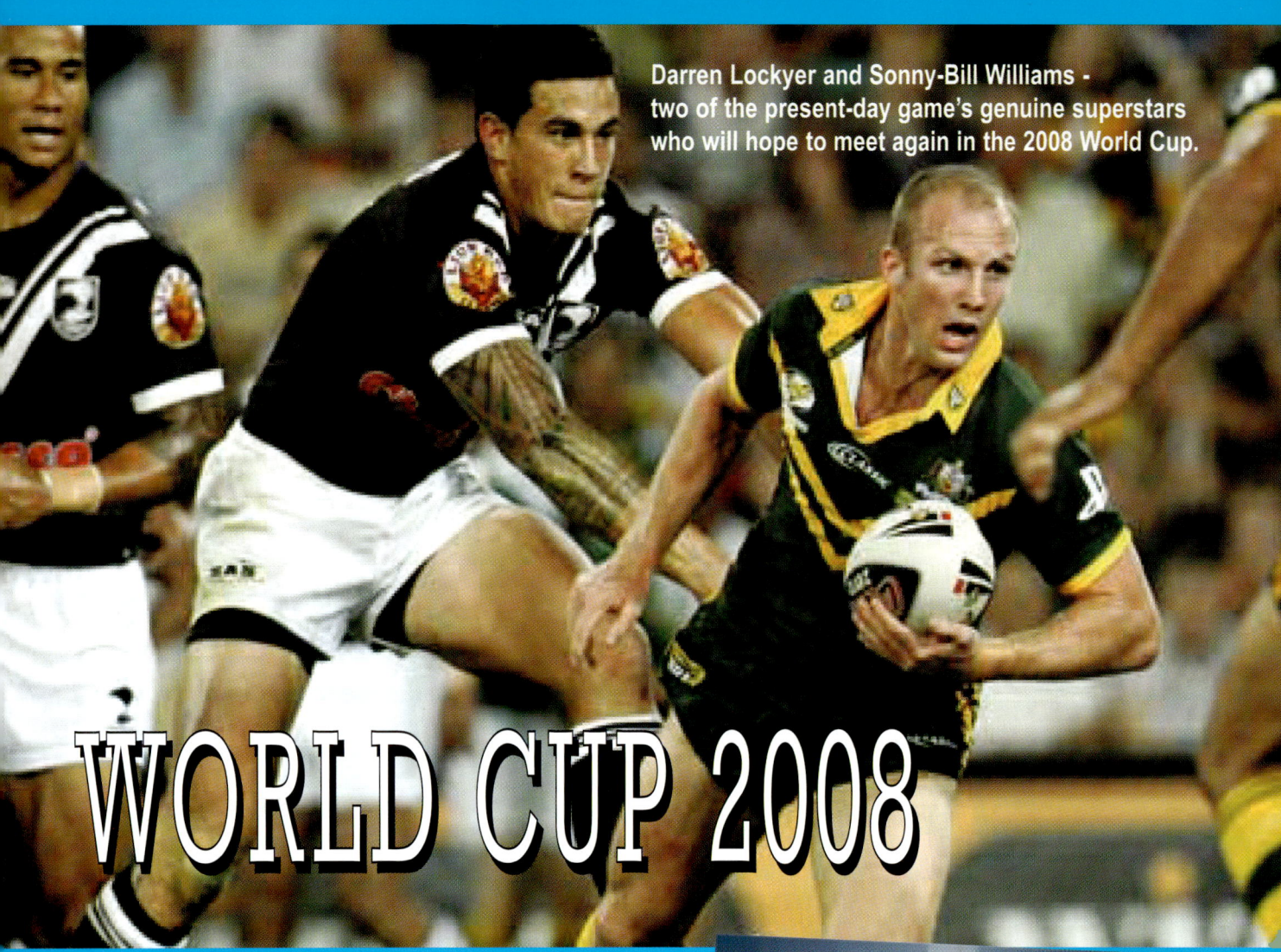

Darren Lockyer and Sonny-Bill Williams - two of the present-day game's genuine superstars who will hope to meet again in the 2008 World Cup.

WORLD CUP 2008

THE thirteenth Rugby League World Cup will be staged in 2008 in Australia. Ten nations will take part in a tournament to help celebrate the centenary of the game in Australia, and with Rugby League currently in such a vibrant state down-under, expectations are very high that this World Cup will be a huge success.

The World Cup is scheduled for after the end of the 2008 season in Australia and will run from 25th October to 22nd November. Games will be played in: Melbourne, Newcastle, Townsville, Gosford, Rockhampton, Canberra, Wollongong, Penrith, Parramatta and on the Gold Coast, in addition to the two major venues of the Sydney Football Stadium and Brisbane's Suncorp Stadium.

Whilst the opening ceremony will be in Sydney on 26th October as a prelude to the massive Australia versus New Zealand match, the tournament officially kicks off a day earlier up in North Queensland at Townsville when England play Papua New Guinea. England's other group games will be against Australia at the Telstra Dome in Melbourne on 2nd November and against New Zealand at Energy Stadium in Newcastle on 8th November. The World Cup Final will be at the Suncorp Stadium (formerly Lang Park) in Brisbane on 22nd November.

Rugby League led the way when it first staged its World Cup in France in 1954, and Great Britain were the first winners.

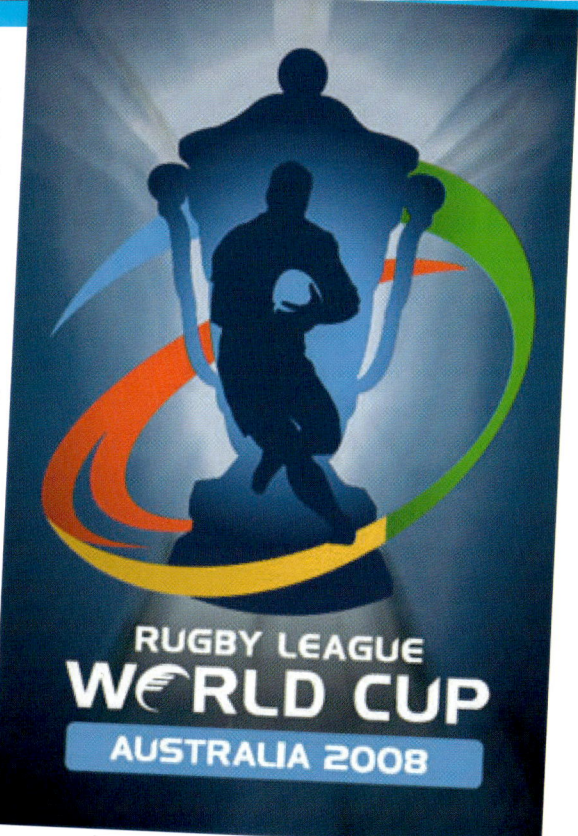

Don't miss your
"RUGBY LEAGUE JOURNAL"
(For Fans Who Don't Want To Forget)

Published quarterly the *"Rugby League Journal"* brings you four issues per year of high quality literature. If you enjoy the nostalgia of looking back on the game you used to know, its players, teams and famous events, with every issue illustrated with a wonderful collection of old black and white photographs all printed on glossy art paper, the *"Rugby League Journal"* is for you. Mixed with analysis and comment on current affairs in the world of Rugby League from writers with vast experience in the game, plus book reviews and obituaries, every issue of the *"Rugby League Journal"* provides a hugely enjoyable mix of history, memorabilia and comment - it is something unique for those who love to remember the game in years gone by.

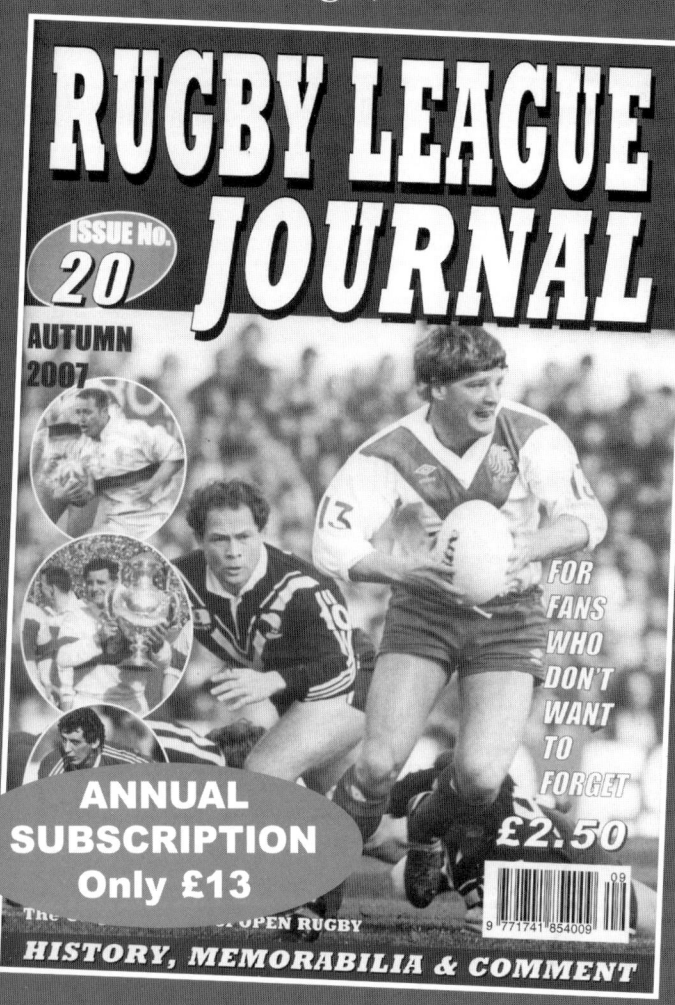

ENSURE YOU DON'T MISS AN ISSUE BY TAKING A SUBSCRIPTION

To book your annual subscription and receive four consecutive issues of the "Journal" just send a cheque or postal order for £13-00 (made payable to *"Rugby League Journal"*), not forgetting to tell us your name and full postal address. Send to:
Rugby League Journal, P.O.Box 22, Egremont, Cumbria, CA23 3WA.
E-mail: rugbyleague.journal@virgin.net   Sales enquiries: Telephone: 01946 814249
(All new suscriptions will be started with the latest issue which is issue number 20 - illustrated above; unless you request to start with another issue.
Individual sample copies available price £3.50 each (including postage & packing)
Overseas subscription rates on request. You can order on-line via secure payment on our web-site.

For more news of "Rugby League Journal" - see our web-site at
www.rugbyleaguejournal.net

Great Britain's Ashes captains

In British Rugby League there has been no higher individual honour for any player than to captain his country in the Ashes against Australia. Since the first ball was kicked in Ashes football back in 1908, thirty-nine series have been played between the two great traditional rivals of Rugby League - with Great Britain winning nineteen and Australia winning twenty. Being captain of a British team in an Ashes series - especially those which were won - has helped create some of the most famous figures in the folklore of the game, among them such as: Harold Wagstaff, Jonty Parkin, Jim Sullivan, Gus Risman, Ernest Ward, Alan Prescott and Eric Ashton. On this page we list every Great Britain captain from every Ashes series.

1908-09 - in England. Bert Jenkins (1); James Lomas (2 and 3)
1910 - in Australia. James Lomas (1 and 2)
* *Only two Tests played.*
1911-12 in England & Scotland. Johnny Thomas (1); James Lomas (2 and 3)
1914 in Australia. Harold Wagstaff (All three Tests)
1920 in Australia. Harold Wagstaff (1 and 3); Gwyn Thomas (2)
1921-22 in England. Harold Wagstaff (1 and 3); Jonty Parkin (2)
1924 in Australia. Jonty Parkin (All three Tests)
1928 in Australia. Jim Sullivan (1 and 3); Jonty Parkin (2)
1929-30 in England. Leslie Fairclough (1); Jonty Parkin (2 and 3); Jim Sullivan (4).
**A fourth Test was played after a drawn series.*
1932 in Australia. Jim Sullivan (All three Tests)
1933 in England. Jim Sullivan (All three Tests)
1936 in Australia. Arthur Atkinson (1); Jim Brough (2); Gus Risman (3)
1937 in England. Gus Risman (All three Tests)
1946 in Australia. Gus Risman (All three Tests)
1948-49 in England. Ernest Ward (All three Tests)
1950 in Australia. Ernest Ward (All three Tests)
1952 in England. Willie Horne (All three Tests)
1954 in Australia. Ernie Ashcroft (1); Dickie Williams (2 and 3).
1956 in England. Alan Prescott (All three Tests)
1958 in Australia. Alan Prescott (1 and 2); Phil Jackson (3)
1959 in England. Eric Ashton (1); Jeff Stevenson (2 and 3)
1962 in Australia. Eric Ashton (All three Tests)
1963 in England. Eric Ashton (1 and 2); Tommy Smales (3)
1966 in Australia. Brian Edgar (All three Tests)
1967 in England. Bill Holliday (All three Tests)
1970 in Australia. Frank Myler (All three Tests)
1973 in England. Clive Sullivan (All three Tests)
1974 in Australia. Chris Hesketh (All three Tests)
1978 in England. Roger Millward (All three Tests)
1979 in Australia. Doug Laughton (1); George Nicholls (2 and 3)

ERNEST WARD of Bradford Northern - one of the most revered of all British captains - who led his country throughout the 1948 and 1950 Ashes series, the first on home soil in England and the second as leader of the Lions in Australia. In later years Ernest served as the Chairman of the British Rugby League Lions Association.

1982 in England. Steve Nash (1); Jeff Grayshon (2); David Topliss (3)
1984 in Australia. Brian Noble (All three Tests)
1986 in England. David Watkinson (All three Tests)
1988 in Australia. Ellery Hanley (All three Tests)
1990 in England. Ellery Hanley (All three Tests)
1992 in Australia. Garry Schofield (All three Tests)
1994 in England. Shaun Edwards (1 and 3); Phil Clarke (2)
2001 in England. Andy Farrell (All three Tests)
2003 in England. Andy Farrell (All three Tests)

GREAT BRITAIN TEST PLAYERS

Martin Offiah, Kevin Ward, Ellery Hanley and Karl Harrison in 1990.

THE COMPLETE REGISTER OF BRITISH INTERNATIONALS

Here and on the following pages we present the complete register of players who have appeared for Great Britain in full Test matches and World Cup games from the first one in 1907-08 to date (i.e. up to and including the June 2007 match versus France played at Headingley, as this book was published before the 2007 home series versus New Zealand was played.) Records in this section do not include matches against France before 1957, the year in which Great Britain-France games were given official Test match status.

KEY: After the player's name we list his total number of Great Britain appearances in brackets with a plus sign indicating substitute appearances, e.g. (5+2); the club(s) he was with, and the years which signify the duration of his G.B. career. *The letters "R.D." indicate the thirteen men who played in the legendary "Rorke's Drift" Test in 1914.*

A

ACKERLEY, Alvin (2) Halifax: 1952-1958.
ADAMS, Les (1) Leeds: 1932.
ADAMS, Mick (11+2) Widnes: 1979-1984.
ANDERSON, Paul (+10) Bradford: 1999 - 2003.
ARKWRIGHT, Chris (+2) St.Helens: 1985.
ARKWRIGHT, Jack (6) Warrington: 1936-1937.
ARMITT, Tommy (8) Swinton: 1933-1937.
ASHBY, Ray (2) Liverpool City & Wigan: 1964 - 1965.
ASHCROFT, Ernest (11) Wigan: 1947 - 1954.

Great Britain Players Register - 2

ASHCROFT, Kevin (5+1) Leigh & Warrington: 1968-1974.
ASHTON, Eric (26) Wigan: 1957-1963.
ASHURST, Bill (3) Wigan: 1971-1972.
ASKIN, Tommy (6) Featherstone Rovers: 1928.
ASPINALL, Willie (1) Warrington: 1966.
ASTON, Len (3) St.Helens: 1947.
ASTON, Mark (+1) Sheffield Eagles: 1991.
ATCHESON, Paul (2+1) St.Helens: 1997.
ATKINSON, Arthur (11) Castleford: 1929-1936.
ATKINSON, John (26) Leeds: 1968-1980.
AVERY, Bert (4) Oldham: 1910-1911

B

BACON, Jim (11) Leeds: 1920-1926.
BAILEY, Ryan (+4) Leeds: 2004.
BARENDS, David (2) Bradford: 1979.
BARTON, Frank (1) Wigan: 1951.
BARTON, John (2) Wigan: 1960-1961.
BASNETT, John (2) Widnes: 1984 - 1986.
BASSETT, Arthur (2) Halifax: 1946.
BATEMAN, Allan (1+2) Warrington: 1992-1994.
BATES, Alan (2+2) Dewsbury: 1974.
BATTEN, Billy (10) Hunslet & Hull: 1907-1921.
BATTEN, Eric (4) Bradford: 1946-1947.
BATTEN, Ray (3) Leeds: 1969-1973.
BAXTER, Johnnie (1) Rochdale Hornets: 1907.
BEAMES, Jack (2) Halifax: 1921.
BEARDMORE, Kevin (13+1) Castleford: 1984-1990.
BELSHAW, Billy (8) Liverpool St. & Warrington: 1936-1937.
BENNETT, Jack (7) Rochdale & Wigan: 1924-1926.
BENTHAM, Billy (2) Broughton Rangers: 1924.
BENTHAM, Nat (10) Wigan Highfield, Halifax and Warrington: 1928-1929.
BENTLEY, John (2) Leeds and Halifax: 1992-1994.
BENTLEY, Keith (1) Widnes: 1980.
BENYON, Billy (5+1) St.Helens: 1971-1972.
BETTS, Denis (30+2) Wigan & Auckland Warr.: 1990-1999.
BEVAN, Dai (1) Wigan: 1952.
BEVAN, John (6) Warrington: 1974-1978.
BEVERLEY, Harry (6) Hunslet & Halifax: 1936-1937.
BIBB, Chris (1) Featherstone Rovers: 1990.
BIRCH, Jim (1) Leeds: 1907.
BISHOP, David (+1) Hull K.R.: 1990.
BISHOP, Tommy (15) St.Helens: 1966-1969.
BLAN, Billy (3) Wigan: 1951.
BLINKHORN, Tom (1) Warrington: 1929.
BOLTON, David (23) Wigan: 1957-1963.
BOSTON, Billy (31) Wigan: 1954-1963.
BOTT, Charlie (1) Oldham: 1966.
BOWDEN, Jim (3) Huddersfield: 1954.
BOWEN, Frank (3) St.Helens Recs.: 1928.
BOWMAN, Eddie (4) Workington Town: 1977.

CHRIS CAMILLERI
Barrow's Welsh winger capped in 1980

BOWMAN, Harold (8) Hull: 1924-1929.
BOWMAN, Ken (3) Huddersfield: 1962-1963.
BOYLEN, Frank (1) Hull: 1908.
BRADSHAW, Tommy (6) Wigan: 1947-1950.
BRIDGES, John "Keith" (3) Featherstone Rovers: 1974.
BRIERS, Lee (1) Warrington: 2001.
BRIGGS, Brian (1) Huddersfield: 1954
BROADBENT, Paul (8) Sheffield Eagles: 1996-1997.
BROGDEN, Stanley (16) Huddersfield & Leeds: 1929-1937.
BROOKE, Ian (13) Bradford & Wakefield: 1966-1968.
BROOKS, Ernest (3) Warrington: 1908.
BROUGH, Albert (2) Oldham: 1924.
BROUGH, Jim (5) Leeds: 1928-1936.
BROWN, Gordon (6) Leeds: 1954-1955.
BRYANT, Bill (4+1) Castleford:1964-1967.
BUCKLEY, Alan (7) Swinton: 1963-1966.
BURGESS, Bill Snr. (16) Barrow: 1924-1929.
BURGESS, Bill Jnr. (14) Barrow: 1962-1969.
BURGHAM, Oliver (1) Halifax: 1911.
BURKE, Mick (14+1) Widnes: 1980-1986.
BURNELL, Alf (3) Hunslet: 1951-1954.
BURROW, Rob (1+1) Leeds: 2005-2007.
BURTON, Chris (8+1) Hull K.R.: 1982-1987.
BURWELL, Alan (7+1) Hull K.R.: 1967-1969.
BUTTERS, Fred (2) Swinton: 1929.

C

CAIRNS, David (2) Barrow: 1984.
CAMILLERI, Chris (2) Barrow: 1980.
CARLTON, Frank (2) St.Helens & Wigan: 1958-1962.
CARNEY, Brian (14) Wigan & Newcastle Knights: 2003-2007.

CARR, Charlie (7) Barrow: 1924-1926.
CARTWRIGHT, Joe (7) Leigh: 1920-1921.
CARVELL, Gareth (+2) Hull: 2007.
CASE, Brian (6+1) Wigan: 1984-1988.
CASEY, Len (12+2) Hull K.R. & Bradford: 1977-1983.
CASSIDY, Mick (1+3) Wigan: 1994-1997.
CASTLE, Frank (4) Barrow: 1952-1954.
CHALLINOR, Jim (3) Warrington: 1958-1960.
CHARLTON, Paul (18+1) Workington & Salford: 1965-1974.
CHERRINGTON, Norman (1) Wigan: 1960.
CHILCOTT, Jack (3) R.D. (Huddersfield): 1914.
CHISNALL, David (2) Leigh: 1970.
CHISNALL, Eric (4) St.Helens: 1974.
CLAMPITT, James (3) Broughton Rangers: 1907-1914.
CLARK, Douglas (11) R.D. Huddersfield: 1911-1920.
CLARK, Garry (3) Hull K.R.: 1984-1985.
CLARK, Mick (5) Leeds: 1968.
CLARKE, Colin (7) Wigan: 1965-1973.
CLARKE, Phil (15+1) Wigan: 1990-1994.
CLAWSON, Terry (14) Featherstone Rovers, Leeds and Oldham: 1962-1974.
CLOSE, Don (1) Huddersfield: 1967.
COLDRICK, Percy (4) R.D. Wigan: 1914.
COLEY, Andy (1) Salford: 2007.
COLLIER, Frank (2) Wigan & Widnes: 1963-1964.
CONNOLLY, Gary (28+3) St.Helens, Wigan and Leeds: 1991-2003.
CORDLE, Gerald (1) Bradford: 1990.
COULMAN, Mike (2+1) Salford: 1971.
COURTNEY, Neil (+1) Warrington: 1982.
COVERDALE, Bob (4) Hull: 1954
COWIE, Neil (3) Wigan: 1993- 1998.
CRACKNELL, Dick (2) Huddrsfield: 1951.
CRANE, Mick (1) Hull: 1982.
CREASSER, David (2+2) Leeds:1985-1988.
CROOKS, Lee (17+2) Hull, Leeds & Castleford: 1982-1994.
CROSTON, Jim (1) Castleford: 1937
CROWTHER, Hector (1) Hunslet: 1929.
CUMMINS, Francis (3) Leeds: 1998-1999.
CUNLIFFE, Billy (11) Warrington: 1920-1926.
CUNLIFFE, Jack (4) Wigan: 1950-1954.
CUNNIFFE, Bernard (1) Castleford: 1937.
CUNNINGHAM, Eddie (1) St.Helens: 1978.
CUNNINGHAM, Keiron (16) St.Helens: 1996-2006.
CURRAN, George (6) Salford: 1946-1948.
CURRIER, Andy (2) Widnes: 1989-1993.
CURZON, Ephraim (1) Salford: 1910.

D

DAGNALL, Bob (4) St.Helens: 1961-1965.
DALGREEN, John (1) Fulham: 1982.
DANBY, Tom (3) Salford: 1950.
DANIELS, Arthur (3) Halifax: 1952-1955.
DANNATT, Andy (3) Hull: 1985-1991.
DARWELL, Joe (5) Leigh: 1924.
DAVIES, Alan (20) Oldham: 1955-1960.

Great Britain Players Register - 3

DAVIES, Billy (1) Swinton: 1968.
DAVIES, Billy J. (1) Castleford: 1933.
DAVIES, Evan (3) Oldham: 1920.
DAVIES, Jim (2) Huddersfield: 1911.
DAVIES, Jonathan (12+1) Widnes & Warrington: 1990-1994.
DAVIES, Will T. (1) Halifax: 1911.
DAVIES, William A. (2) *R.D.* Leeds: 1914.
DAVIES, Willie T.H. (3) Bradford: 1946-1947.
DAWSON, Edgar (1) York: 1956.
DEACON, Paul (10+1) Bradford: 2001-2005.
DERMOTT, Martin (11) Wigan: 1990-1993.
DEVEREUX, John (6+2) Widnes: 1992-1993.
DICK, Kevin (2) Leeds: 1980.
DICKENSON, George (1) Warrington: 1908.
DICKINSON, Roy (2) Leeds: 1985.
DINGSDALE, Billy (3) Warrington: 1929-1933.
DISKIN, Matt (1) Leeds: 2004.
DIVORTY, Gary (2) Hull: 1985.
DIXON, Colin (12+2) Halifax & Salford: 1968 - 1974.
DIXON, Malcolm (2) Featherstone Rovers: 1962 - 1964.
DIXON, Paul (11+4) Halifax & Leeds: 1987 - 1992.
DOCKAR, Alec (1) Hull K.R.: 1947.
DONLAN, Steve (+2) Leigh: 1984.
DRAKE, Bill (1) Hull: 1962
DRAKE, Jim (1) Hull: 1960.
DRUMMOND, Des (24) Leigh & Warrington: 1980 - 1988.
DUANE, Ronnie (3) Warrington: 1983 - 1984.
DUTTON, Ray (6) Widnes: 1970.
DWYER, Bernard (+1) Bradford: 1996.
DYL, Les (11) Leeds: 1974 - 1982.
DYSON, Frank (1) Huddersfield: 1959.

E

EASTWOOD, Paul (13) Hull: 1990 - 1992.
ECCLES, Bob (1) Warrington: 1982.
ECCLES, Percy (1) Halifax: 1907.
ECKERSLEY, David (2+2) St.Helens: 1973 - 1974.
EDGAR, Brian (11) Workington Town: 1958 - 1966.
EDWARDS, Alan (7) Salford: 1936 - 1937.
EDWARDS, Derek (3+2) Castleford: 1968 - 1971.
EDWARDS, Shaun (32+4) Wigan: 1985 - 1994.
EGAN, Joe (14) Wigan: 1946 - 1950.
ELLABY, Alf (13) St.Helens: 1928 - 1933.
ELLIS, Gareth (11+3) Wakefield Trinity & Leeds: 2003 - 2007.
ELLIS, Kevin (+1) Warrington: 1991.
ELLIS, St.John (+3) Castleford: 1991-1994.
ELWELL, Keith (3) Widnes: 1977 - 1980.
ENGLAND, Keith (6+5) Castleford: 1987 - 1991.
EVANS, Bryn (10) Swinton: 1926 - 1933.

EVANS, Frank (4) Swinton: 1924.
EVANS, Jack (4) Hunslet: 1951- 1952.
EVANS, Jack (3) Swinton: 1926.
EVANS, Roy (4) Wigan: 1961 - 1962.
EVANS, Steve (7+3) Featherstone & Hull: 1979 - 1982.
EYRE, Ken (1) Hunslet: 1965.
EYRES, Richard (3+6) Widnes: 1989 - 1993.

F

FAIRBAIRN, George (17) Wigan & Hull K.R.: 1977 - 1982.
FAIRBANK, Karl (10+6) Bradford: 1987 - 1994.
FAIRCLOUGH, Les (6) St.Helens: 1926 - 1929.
FARRAR, Vince (1) Hull: 1978.
FARRELL, Andrew (34) Wigan: 1993 - 2004.
FEATHERSTONE, Jimmy (6) Warrington: 1948 - 1952.
FEETHAM, Jack (8) Hull K.R. & Salford: 1929 - 1933.
FIELD, Harry (3) York: 1936.
FIELD, Norman (1) Batley: 1963.
FIELDEN, Stuart (22+3) Bradford & Wigan: 2001 - 2007.
FIELDHOUSE, John (7) Widnes & St.Helens: 1985 - 1986.
FIELDING, Keith (3) Salford: 1974 - 1977.
FILDES, Alec (15) St.Helens Recs. & St.Helens: 1926 - 1932.
FISHER, Tony (11) Bradford & Leeds: 1970 - 1978.
FLANAGAN, Peter (14) Hull K.R.: 1962 - 1970.
FLANAGAN, Terry (4) Oldham: 1983 - 1984.
FLEARY, Darren (1+1) Leeds: 1998.
FOGERTY, Terry (2+1) Halifax, Wigan & RochdaleHornets: 1966 - 1974.

FORD, Michael (+2) Castleford: 1993.
FORD, Phil (13) Wigan, Bradford & Leeds: 1985 - 1989.
FORSHAW, Mike (8+6) Bradford: 1997 - 2003.
FORSTER, Mark (2) Warrington: 1987.
FOSTER, Frank (1) Hull K.R.: 1967.
FOSTER, Peter (3) Leigh: 1955.
FOSTER, Trevor (3) Bradford: 1946 - 1948.
FOX, Deryck (10+4) Featherstone & Bradford: 1985 - 1992.
FOX, Don (1) Featherstone Rovers: 1963.
FOX, Neil (29) Wakefield Trinity: 1959 - 1969.
FOY, Des (3) Oldham: 1984 - 1985.
FOZZARD, Nick (+1) St.Helens: 2005.
FRANCIS, Bill (4) Wigan: 1967 - 1977.
FRANCIS, Roy (1) Barrow: 1947.
FRASER, Eric (16) Warrington: 1958 - 1961.
FRENCH, Ray (4) Widnes: 1968.
FRODSHAM, Alf (3) St.Helens: 1928 - 1929.

G

GABBITAS, Brian (1) Hunslet: 1959.
GALLAGHER, Frank (12) Dewsbury & Batley: 1920 - 1926.
GANLEY, Bernard (3) Oldham: 1957 - 1958.
GARDINER, Danny (1) Wigan: 1965.
GARDNER, Ade (2) St.Helens: 2006 - 2007.
GEE, Ken (17) Wigan: 1946 - 1951.
GEMMELL, Dick (3) Leeds & Hull: 1964 - 1969.
GIBSON, Carl (10+1) Batley & Leeds: 1985 - 1991.
GIFFORD, Harry (2) Barrow: 1908.
GILFEDDER, Laurie (5) Warrington: 1962 - 1963.
GILL, Henderson (14+1) Wigan: 1981- 1988
GILL, Ken (5+2) Salford: 1974 - 1977.

JOE EGAN, MARTIN RYAN, JOHNNY LAWRENSON, KEN GEE, GEORGE CURRAN.
Five Wiganers in the Great Britain team during the 1948 Ashes series in England.

Great Britain Players Register - 4

GILMOUR, Lee (5+9) Wigan, Bradford & St.Helens: 1998 - 2007.
GLEESON, Martin (16+1) St.Helens & Warrington: 2002 - 2007.
GOODWAY, Andy (23) Oldham & Wigan: 1983 - 1990.
GOODWIN, Dennis (5) Barrow: 1957-1958
GORE, Jack (1) Salford: 1926.
GORLEY, Les (4+1) Widnes: 1980 -1982.
GORLEY, Peter (2+1) St.Helens:1980-1981.
GOULDING, Bobbie (13+2) Wigan, Leeds & St.Helens: 1990 - 1997.
GOWERS, Ken (14) Swinton: 1962 - 1966.
GRAHAM, James (+2) St.Helens: 2006-2007.
GRAY, John (5+3) Wigan: 1974.
GRAYSHON, Jeff (13) Bradford & Leeds: 1979 - 1985.
GREENALL, Doug (6) St.Helens:1951-1954.
GREENALL, Johnny (1) St.Helens Recs.: 1921.
GREENHOUGH, Bobby (1) Warrington: 1960.
GREGORY, Andy (25+1) Widnes, Warrington & Wigan: 1981 - 1992.
GREGORY, Mike (19+1) Warrington: 1987 - 1990.
GRIBBIN, Vince (1) Whitehaven: 1985.
GRIFFITHS, Jonathan (1) St.Helens: 1992.
GRONOW, Ben (7) Huddersfield: 1911 - 1920.
GROVES, Paul (1) St.Helens: 1987.
GRUNDY, Jack (12) Barrow: 1955 - 1957.
GUNNEY, Geoff (11) Hunslet: 1954 - 1965.
GWYNNE, Emlyn (3) Hull: 1929 - 1929.
GWYTHER, Elwyn (6) Belle Vue Rangers: 1947 - 1951.

H

HAGGERTY, Roy (2) St.Helens: 1987.
HAIGH, Bob (5+1) Wakefield & Leeds: 1968 - 1971.
HALL, Billy (4) *R.D.* Oldham: 1914.
HALL, David (2) Hull K.R.: 1984.
HALLAS, Derek (2) Leeds: 1961.

BRIAN LOCKWOOD & STEVE NORTON
Forwards in the 1978 Ashes series

HALMSHAW, Tony (1) Halifax: 1971.
HALSALL, Hector (1) Swinton: 1929.
HAMMOND, Karle (1+1) St.Helens: 1996.
HAMPSON, Steve (11+1) Wigan: 1987 - 1992.
HANLEY, Ellery (35+1) Bradford, Wigan & Leeds: 1984 - 1993.
HARDISTY, Alan (12) Castleford: 1964 - 1970.
HARE, Ian (1) Widnes: 1967.
HARKIN, Paul (+1) Hull K.R.: 1985.
HARRIS, Iestyn (12+3) Warrington, Leeds & Bradford: 1996 - 2005.
HARRIS, Tommy (25) Hull: 1954 - 1960.
HARRISON, Fred (3) Leeds: 1911.
HARRISON, Karl (11+5) Hull & Halifax: 1990 - 1994.
HARRISON, Mick (7) Hull: 1967 - 1973.
HARTLEY, Dennis (11) Hunslet & Castleford: 1964 - 1970.
HARTLEY, Steve (3) Hull K.R.: 1980 - 1981.
HAUGHTON, Simon (+5) Wigan: 1997 - 1998.
HAY, Andy (+2) Leeds: 1999.
HAYES, Joey (1) St.Helens: 1996.
HELME, Gerry (12) Warrington: 1948 - 1954.
HEPWORTH, Keith (11) Castleford: 1967 - 1970.
HERBERT, Norman (6) Workington Town: 1961 - 1962.
HERON, David (1+1) Leeds: 1982.
HESKETH, Chris (21+2) Salford: 1970 - 1974.
HICKS, Mervyn (1) St.Helens: 1965.
HIGGINS, Fred (6) Widnes: 1950 - 1951.
HIGGINS, Harold (2) Widnes: 1937.
HIGHAM, Micky (+4) St.Helens: 2004 - 2005.
HIGSON, John (2) Hunslet: 1908.
HILL, Cliff (1) Wigan: 1966.
HILL, David (1) Wigan: 1971.
HILTON, Herman (7) Oldham: 1920 - 1921.
HILTON, Jack (4) Wigan: 1950.
HOBBS, David (10+2) Featherstone, Oldham & Bradford: 1984 - 1989.
HOCK, Gareth (3+1) Wigan: 2007.
HODGSON, David (2+1) Wigan & Salford: 2001 - 2007.
HODGSON, Martin (16) Swinton: 1929 - 1937.
HOGAN, Phil (6+3) Barrow & Hull K.R.: 1977 - 1979.
HOGG, Andrew (1) Broughton Rangers: 1907.
HOLDEN, Keith (1) Warrington: 1963.
HOLDER, Billy (1) Hull: 1907.
HOLDING, Neil (4) St.Helens: 1984.
HOLDSTOCK, Roy (2) Hull K.R.: 1980.
HOLLAND, David (4) *R.D.* Oldham: 1914.
HOLLIDAY, Bill (9+1) Whitehaven & Hull K.R.: 1964 - 1967.
HOLLIDAY, Les (3) Widnes: 1991 - 1992.
HOLLINDRAKE, Terry (1) Keighley: 1955.
HOLMES, John (14+6) Leeds: 1971 - 1982.
HORNE, Richard (5+6) Hull: 2001 - 2007.

HORNE, Willie (8) Barrow: 1946 - 1952.
HORTON, Bill (14) Wakefield Trinity: 1928 - 1933.
HOWARD, Harvey (+1) Bradford: 1998.
HUDDART, Dick (16) Whitehaven & St.Helens: 1958 - 1963.
HUDSON, Barney (8) Salford: 1932 - 1937.
HUDSON, Bill (1) Wigan: 1948.
HUGHES, Eric (8) Widnes: 1978 - 1982.
HULME, David (7+1) Widnes: 1988 - 1989.
HULME, Paul (3+5) Widnes: 1988 - 1992.
HUNTE, Alan (15) St.Helens: 1992 - 1997.
HURCOMBE, Danny (8) Wigan: 1920 - 1924.
HYNES, Syd (12+1) Leeds: 1970 -1973.

I

IRVING, Bob (8+3) Oldham: 1967 - 1972.
IRWIN, Shaun (+4) Castleford: 1990.

J

JACKSON, Ken (2) Oldham: 1957.
JACKSON, Lee (17) Hull & Sheffield Eagles : 1990 - 1994.
JACKSON, Michael (2+4) Wakefield & Halifax: 1991 - 1993.
JACKSON, Phil (27) Barrow: 1954 - 1958.
JAMES, Neil (1) Halifax: 1986.
JARMAN, Billy (2) Leeds: 1914.
JASIEWICZ, Dick (1) Bradford: 1984.
JEANES, David (8) Wakefield & Leeds: 1971 - 1972.
JENKINS, Bert (12) Wigan: 1907 - 1914.
JENKINS, Dai (1) Hunslet: 1929.
JENKINS, Dai (1) Hunslet: 1947.
JENKINS, Emlyn (9) Salford: 1933 - 1937.
JENKINSON, Albert (2) Hunslet: 1911.
JOHNSON, Albert (4) *R.D.* Widnes: 1914 - 1920.
JOHNSON, Albert (6) Warrington: 1946 - 1947.
JOHNSON, Chris (1) Leigh: 1985.
JOHNSON, Paul (9+4) Wigan & Bradford: 2001 - 2005.
JOLLEY, Jim (3) Runcorn: 1907
JONES, Berwyn (3) Wakefield Trinity: 1964 - 1966.
JONES, Dai (2) Merthyr: 1907.
JONES, Ernest (4) Rochdale Hornets: 1920.
JONES, Joe (1) Barrow: 1946.
JONES, Keri (2) Wigan: 1970.
JONES, Les (1) St.Helens: 1971.
JONES, Lewis (15) Leeds: 1954 - 1957.
JONES, Mark (+1) Hull: 1992.
JORDAN, Gary (2) Featherstone Rovers: 1964 - 1967.
JOYNER, John (14+2) Castleford: 1978 - 1984.
JOYNT, Chris (19+6) St.Helens: 1993 - 2002.
JUBB, Ken (2) Leeds: 1937.
JUKES, Bill (6) Hunslet: 1908 - 1910.

K

KARALIUS, Tony (4+1) St.Helens: 1971 - 1972.

Great Britain Players Register - 5

KARALIUS, Vince (12) St.Helens & Widnes: 1958 - 1963.
KEEGAN, Arthur (9) Hull: 1966 - 1969.
KELLY, Ken (4) St.Helens & Warrington: 1972 - 1982.
KEMEL, George (2) Widnes: 1965.
KERSHAW, Herbert (2) Wakefield Trinity: 1910.
KING, Paul (1) Hull: 2001.
KINNEAR, Roy (1) Wigan: 1929.
KISS, Nicky (1) Wigan: 1985.
KITCHEN, Frank (2) Leigh: 1954.
KITCHIN, Philip (1) Whitehaven: 1965.
KITCHING, Jack (1) Bradford: 1946.
KNAPMAN, Ernest (1) Oldham: 1924.
KNOWELDEN, Bryn (1) Barrow: 1946.

L

LANGLEY, Jamie (+1) Bradford: 2007.
LAUGHTON, Dale (4+1) Sheffield Eagles: 1998 - 1999.
LAUGHTON, Doug (15) Wigan & Widnes: 1970 - 1979.
LAWRENSON, Johnny (3) Wigan: 1948.
LAWS, David (1) Hull K.R.: 1986.
LEDGARD, Jim (11) Dewsbury & Leigh: 1947 - 1954.
LEDGER, Barry (2) St.Helens: 1985 - 1986.
LEWIS, Gordon (1) Leigh: 1965.
LEYTHAM, Jim (5) Wigan: 1907 - 1910.
LITTLE, Syd (10) Oldham: 1956 - 1958.
LLEWELLYN, Tom (2) Oldham: 1907.
LLOYD, Robbie (1) Halifax: 1920.
LOCKWOOD, Brian (8+1) Castleford & Hull K.R.:1972 - 1979.
LOMAS, Jim (7) Salford & Oldham: 1908 - 1911.
LONG, Sean (10+5) St.Helens: 1997 - 2007.
LONGSTAFF, Fred (2) Huddersfield: 1914.
LONGWORTH, Bill (3) Oldham: 1908.
LOUGHLIN, Paul (14+1) St.Helens: 1988 - 1992.
LOWE, John (1) Leeds: 1932.
LOWE, Phil (12) Hull K.R.: 1970 - 1978.
LOWES, James (5) Bradford: 1997 - 2002.
LOXTON, Ken (1) Huddersfield: 1971.
LUCAS, Ian (1+1) Wigan: 1991 - 1992.
LYDON, Joe (23+7) Widnes & Wigan: 1983 - 1992.
LYNCH, Andy (1) Bradford: 2007.

M

McCORMICK, Stan (3) Belle Vue Rangers & St.Helens: 1948.
McCUE, Tommy (6) Widnes: 1936 - 1946.
McCURRIE, Steve (1) Widnes: 1993.
McDERMOTT, Barrie (11+3) Wigan & Leeds: 1994 - 2003.
McDERMOTT, Brian (4) Bradford: 1996 - 1997.
McGINTY, Billy (4) Wigan: 1992.
McGUIRE, Danny (8+2) Leeds: 2004- 2007.
McINTYRE, Len (1) Oldham: 1963.
McKEATING, Vince (2) Workington Town: 1951.

VINCE KARALIUS "The Wild Bull of the Pampas" - in action for Great Britain on the 1958 tour.

McKINNEY, Tom (11) Salford, Warrington & St.Helens: 1951 - 1957.
McNAMARA, Steve (+4) Hull & Bradford: 1992 - 1997.
McTIGUE, Brian (25) Wigan: 1958 - 1963.
MANN, Arthur (2) Bradford: 1908.
MANTLE, John (13) St.Helens: 1966 - 1973.
MARCHANT, Tony (3) Castleford: 1986.
MARTIN, Bill (1) Workington Town: 1962.
MARTYN, Mick (2) Leigh: 1958 -1959.
MATHER, Barrie-Jon (1+2) Wigan & Perth Reds: 1994 - 1996.
MATHIAS, Roy (1) St.Helens: 1979.
MEASURES, Jim (2) Widnes: 1963.
MEDLEY, Paul (3+1) Leeds: 1987 - 1988.
MELLING, Chris (1) Harlequins: 2007.
MIDDLETON, Alf (1) Salford: 1929.
MILLER, Joe (1) Wigan: 1911.
MILLER, Joe "Jack" (6) Warrington: 1933 -1936.
MILLS, Jim (6) Widnes: 1974 - 1979.
MILLWARD, Roger (28+1) Castleford & Hull K.R.:1966 - 1978.
MILNES, Alf (2) Halifax: 1920.
MOLLOY, Steve (2+2) Leeds & Featherstone: 1993 - 1996.
MOONEY, Walter (2) Leigh: 1924.
MOORHOUSE, Stanley (2) Huddersfield: 1914.
MORGAN, Arnold (4) Featherstone Rovers: 1968.
MORGAN, Edgar (2) Hull: 1921.
MORGAN, Ron (2) Swinton: 1963.
MORIARTY, Paul (1+1) Widnes: 1991 - 1994.
MORLEY, Adrian (21+6) Leeds, Sydney Roosters & Warrington: 1996- 2007.
MORLEY, Jack (2) Wigan: 1936 - 1937.
MORTIMER, Frank (2) Wakefield: 1956.
MOSES, Glyn (9) St.Helens: 1955 - 1957.
MUMBY, Keith (11) Bradford: 1982 - 1984.
MURPHY, Alex (27) St.Helens & Warrington: 1958 - 1971.
MURPHY, Harry (1) Wakefield Trinity: 1950.
MYLER, Frank (23+1) Widnes & St.Helens: 1960 - 1970.
MYLER, Tony (14) Widnes: 1983 - 1986.

N

NASH, Steve (24) Featherstone & Salford: 1971 - 1982.
NAUGHTON, Albert (2) Warrington: 1954.

Great Britain Players Register - 6

NEWBOULD, **Tommy** (1) Wakefield Trinity: 1910.
NEWLOVE, **Paul** (16+4) Featherstone, Bradford & St.Helens: 1989 - 1998.
NEWTON, **Terry** (12+2) Leeds, Wigan & Bradford: 1998 - 2007.
NICHOLLS, **George** (29) Widnes & St.Helens: 1971 - 1979.
NICHOLSON, **Bob** (3) Huddersfield: 1946 - 1948.
NICKLE, **Sonny** (1+5) St.Helens: 1992 - 1994.
NOBLE, **Brian** (11) Bradford: 1982 - 1984.
NORTON, **Steve** (11+1) Castleford & Hull: 1974 - 1982.

O

O'CONNOR, **Terry** (11+2) Wigan: 1996 - 2002.
OFFIAH, **Martin** (33) Widnes & Wigan: 1988 - 1994.
O'GRADY, **Terry** (6) Oldham & Warrington: 1954 -1961.
OLIVER, **Joe** (4) Batley: 1928.
O'LOUGHLIN, **Sean** (4+4) Wigan: 2004 - 2007.
O'NEILL, **Dennis** (2+1) Widnes: 1971 - 1972.
O'NEILL, **Mike** (3) Widnes: 1982 -1983.
ORR, **Danny** (+2) Castleford: 2002.
OSTER, **Jack** (1) Oldham: 1929.
OWEN, **Jim** (1) St.Helens Recs.: 1921.
OWEN, **Stan** (1) Leigh: 1958.
OWENS, **Ike** (4) Leeds: 1946.

P

PADBURY, **Dick** (1) Runcorn: 1908.
PALIN, **Harold** (2) Warrington: 1947.
PARKER, **Dave** (2) Oldham: 1964.
PARKIN, **Jonathan** (17) Wakefield Trinity: 1920 - 1929.
PARR, **Ken** (1) Warrington: 1968.
PAWSEY, **Charlie** (7) Leigh: 1952 - 1954.
PEACOCK, **Jamie** (20+3) Bradford & Leeds: 2001 - 2007.
PEPPERELL, **Albert** (2) Workington Town: 1950 -1951.
PHILLIPS, **Doug** (4) Oldham & Belle Vue R.: 1946 - 1950.
PHILLIPS, **Rowland** (+1) Workington Town: 1996.
PIMBLETT, **Albert** (3) Warrington: 1948.
PINNER, **Harry** (6+1) St.Helens: 1980 - 1986.
PITCHFORD, **Frank** (2) Oldham: 1958 - 1962.
PITCHFORD, **Steve** (4) Leeds: 1977.
PLANGE, **David** (1) Castleford: 1988.
PLATT, **Andy** (21+4) St.Helens & Wigan: 1985 - 1993.
POLLARD, **Charlie** (1) Wakefield Trinity: 1924.
POLLARD, **Ernest** (2) Wakefield Trinity: 1932.
POLLARD, **Roy** (1) Dewsbury: 1950.
POOLE, **Harry** (3) Hull K.R.: 1964 - 1966.

POTTER, **Ian** (7+1) Wigan: 1985 - 1986.
POWELL, **Daryl** (23+10) Sheffield & Keighley: 1990 - 1996.
POWELL, **Roy** (13+6) Leeds: 1985 - 1991.
POYNTON, **Harold** (3) Wakefield Trinity: 1962.
PRATT, **Karl** (2) Leeds: 2002.
PRESCOTT, **Alan** (28) St.Helens: 1951 - 1958.
PRICE, **Gary H.** (+1) Wakefield Trinity: 1991.
PRICE, **Jack** (6) Broughton Rangers & Wigan: 1921 - 1924.
PRICE, **Malcolm** (2) Rochdale Hornets: 1967.
PRICE, **Ray** (9) Warrington: 1954 - 1957.
PRICE, **Terry** (1) Bradford: 1970.
PRIOR, **Bernard** (1) Hunslet: 1966.
PROCTOR, **Wayne** (+1) Hull: 1984.
PROSSER, **Dai** (1) Leeds: 1937.
PROSSER, **Stuart** (1) *R.D.* Halifax: 1914.
PRYCE, **Leon** (15) Bradford & St.Helens: 2001 - 2007.

R

RADLINSKI, **Kris** (20) Wigan: 1996 - 2003.
RAE, **Johnny** (1) Bradford: 1965.
RAMSDALE, **Dick** (8) *R.D.* Wigan: 1910 - 1914.
RAMSEY, **Bill** (7+1) Hunslet & Bradford: 1965 - 1974.
RATCLIFFE, **Gordon** (3) Wigan: 1947-1950.
RATHBONE, **Alan** (4+1) Bradford: 1982 - 1985.
RAYNE, **Keith** (4) Leeds: 1984.
RAYNE, **Kevin** (1) Leeds: 1986.
RAYNOR, **Gareth** (4) Hull: 2005 - 2007.
REARDON, **Stuart** (5) Bradford: 2004.
REDFEARN, **Alan** (1) Bradford: 1979.
REDFEARN, **David** (6+1) Bradford: 1972 - 1974.
REES, **Billo** (11) Swinton: 1926 - 1929.
REES, **Dai** (1) Halifax: 1926.

REES, **Tom** (1) Oldham: 1929.
REILLY, **Malcolm** (9) Castleford: 1970.
RENILSON, **Charlie** (7+1) Halifax: 1965 - 1968.
RHODES, **Austin** (4) St.Helens: 1957 - 1961.
RICHARDS, **Maurice** (2) Salford: 1974.
RILEY, **Joe** (1) Halifax: 1910.
RING, **Johnny** (2) Wigan: 1924- 1926.
RISMAN, **Bev** (5) Leeds: 1968.
RISMAN, **Gus** (17) Salford: 1932 - 1946.
RIX, **Sid** (9) Oldham: 1924 -1926.
ROBERTS, **Ken** (10) Halifax: 1963 - 1966.
ROBINSON, **Asa** (3) Halifax: 1907 -1908.
ROBINSON, **Dave** (13) Swinton & Wigan: 1965 - 1970.
ROBINSON, **Bill** (2) Leigh: 1963.
ROBINSON, **Don** (10) Wakefield & Leeds: 1954 - 1960.
ROBINSON, **Jack** (2) Rochdale Hornets: 1914.
ROBINSON, **Jason** (12) Wigan: 1993 - 1999.
ROBY, **James** (1+4) St.Helens: 2007.
ROGERS, **Johnny** (7) Huddersfield 1914 - 1921.
ROSE, **David** (4) Leeds: 1954.
ROSE, **Paul** (2+3) Hull K.R. & Hull: 1974 - 1982.
ROUND, **Gerry** (8) Wakefield Trinity 1959 - 1962.
RUDDICK, **George** (3) Broughton Rangers: 1907 - 1910.
RYAN, **Bob** (5) Warrington: 1950 - 1952.
RYAN, **Martin** (4) Wigan: 1947 - 1950.
RYDER, **Ron** (1) Warrington: 1952.

S

SAMPSON, **Dean** (+1) Castleford: 1997.
SAYER, **Bill** (7) Wigan: 1961 - 1963.
SCHOFIELD, **Derrick** (1) Halifax: 1955.
SCHOFIELD, **Garry** (44-2) Hull & Leeds: 1984 - 1994.
SCULTHORPE, **Paul** (24+2) Warrington & St.Helens: 1996 - 2006.
SEABOURNE, **Barry** (1) Leeds: 1970.
SENIOR, **Keith** (28+2) Sheffield Eagles & Leeds: 1996 - 2007.
SENIOR, **Ken** (2) Huddersfield: 1965 - 1967.
SHARROCK, **Jim** (4) Wigan: 1910 - 1911.
SHAW, **Brian** (5) Hunslet & Leeds: 1956 - 1961.
SHAW, **Glyn** (1) Widnes: 1980.
SHAW, **John "Joby"** (5) Halifax: 1960 - 1962.
SHELTON, **Geoff** (7) Hunslet: 1964 - 1966.
SHERIDAN, **Ryan** (3) Leeds: 1999 - 2002.
SHOEBOTTOM, **Mick** (10+2) Leeds: 1968 - 1971.
SHUGARS, **Frank** (1) Warrington: 1910.
SILCOCK, **Dick** (1) Wigan: 1908.
SILCOCK, **Nat Snr.** (12) Widnes: 1932 - 1937.
SILCOCK, **Nat Jnr.** (3) Wigan: 1954.
SIMMS, **Barry** (1) Leeds: 1962.
SINFIELD, **Kevin** (6+7) Leeds: 2001 - 2007

KEN TRAILL and WILLIE HORNE meet Lord Derby before a 1952 Test.

Great Britain Players Register - 7

SKELHORNE, George "Jack" (7) Warrington: 1920 - 1921.
SKERRETT, Kelvin (14+2) Bradford & Wigan: 1989 - 1993.
SKERRETT, Trevor (10) Wakefield & Hull: 1979 - 1982.
SLOMAN, Bob (3) Oldham: 1928.
SMALES, Tommy (8) Huddersfield & Bradford: 1962 - 1965.
SMALL, Peter (1) Castleford: 1962.
SMITH, Alan (10) Leeds: 1970 - 1973.
SMITH, Arthur (6) Oldham: 1907 - 1908.
SMITH, Bert (2) Bradford: 1926.
SMITH, Fred (9) *R.D.* Hunslet: 1910 -1914.
SMITH, Geoff (3) York: 1963 - 1964.
SMITH, Mike (10+1) Hull K.R.: 1979 - 1984.
SMITH, Peter (1+5) Featherstone Rovers: 1977 - 1984.
SMITH, Sam (4) Hunslet: 1954.
SMITH, Stanley (11) Wakefield Trinity: 1929 - 1933.
SMITH, Tony (3+2) Castleford & Wigan: 1996 - 1998.
SOUTHWARD, Ike (11) Workington & Oldham: 1958 - 1962.
SPENCER, Jack (1) Salford: 1907.
SPRUCE, Stuart (6) Widnes & Bradford: 1993 - 1996.
STACEY, Cyril (1) Hunslet: 1920.
STEADMAN, Graham (9+1) Castleford: 1990 -1994.
STEPHENS, Gary (5) Castleford: 1979.
STEPHENSON, David (9+1) Wigan & Leeds: 1982 - 1988.
STEPHENSON, Mike (5+1) Dewsbury: 1971 - 1972.
STEVENSON, Jeff (19) Leeds & York: 1955 - 1960.
STOCKWELL, Squire (3) Leeds: 1920 - 1921.
STONE, Billy (8) Hull: 1920 -1921.
STOPFORD, John (12) Swinton: 1961 - 1966.
STOTT, Jim (1) St.Helens: 1947.
STREET, Harry (4) Dewsbury: 1950.
SULLIVAN, Anthony (7) St.Helens: 1991 - 1999.
SULLIVAN, Clive (17) Hull: 1967 - 1973.
SULLIVAN, Jim (25) Wigan: 1924 - 1933.
SULLIVAN, Mick (46) Huddersfield, Wigan, St.Helens & York: 1954 - 1963.
SYKES, Paul (1) Harlequins: 2007.
SZYMALA, Eddie (1+1) Barrow: 1981.

T

TAIT, Alan (10+4) Widnes & Leeds: 1989 - 1993.
TAYLOR, Bob (2) Hull: 1921 -1926.
TAYLOR, Harry (3) Hull: 1907.
TEMBEY, John (2) St.Helens: 1963 - 1964.
TERRY, Abe (11) St.Helens & Leeds: 1958 - 1962.
THACKRAY, Jamie (+3) Hull: 2005.
THOMAS, Arthur "Ginger" (4) Leeds: 1926 - 1929.
THOMAS, George (1) Warrington: 1907.

THOMAS, Gwyn (9) Wigan & Huddersfield: 1914 - 1921.
THOMAS, Johnny (8) Wigan: 1907 - 1911.
THOMAS, Les (1) Oldham: 1947.
THOMAS, Phil (1) Leeds: 1907.
THOMPSON, Cec (2) Hunslet: 1951.
THOMPSON, Jimmy (20+1) Featherstone & Bradford: 1970 - 1978.
THOMPSON, Joe (12) Leeds: 1924 - 1932.
THORLEY, John (4) Halifax: 1954.
TOOHEY, Ted (3) Barrow: 1952.
TOPLISS, David (4) Wakefield Trinity & Hull: 1973 - 1982.
TRAILL, Ken (8) Bradford: 1950 - 1954.
TROUP, Alec (2) Barrow: 1936.
TURNBULL, Drew (1) Leeds: 1951.
TURNER, Derek (24) Oldham & Wakefield: 1956 - 1962.
TYSON, Brian (3) Hull K.R.: 1963 - 1967.
TYSON, George (4) Oldham: 1907 - 1908.

V

VALENTINE, Dave (15) Huddersfield: 1948 - 1954.
VALENTINE, Rob (1) Huddersfield: 1967.
VINES, Don (3) Wakefield Trinity: 1959.

W

WADDELL, Hugh (5) Oldham & Leeds: 1988 - 1989.
WAGSTAFF, Harold (12) *R.D.* Huddersfield: 1911 - 1921.
WALKER, Arnold (1) Whitehaven: 1980.
WALKER, Chev (+6) Leeds: 2004 - 2005.
WALLACE, Jim (1) St.Helens Recs.: 1926.
WALSH, Joe (1) Leigh: 1971.
WALSH, John (4+1) St.Helens: 1972.
WALTON, Doug (1) Castleford: 1965.
WANE, Shaun (2) Wigan: 1985 - 1986.
WARD, Billy (1) Leeds: 1910.
WARD, Danny (+1) Leeds: 2004.
WARD, David (12) Leeds: 1977 - 1982.
WARD, Ernest (20) Bradford: 1946 - 1952.
WARD, Johnny (4) Castleford & Salford: 1963 - 1970.
WARD, Kevin (15+2) Castleford & St.Helens: 1984 - 1992.
WARD, Ted (3) Wigan: 1946 - 1947.
WARLOW, John (6+1) St.Helens & Widnes: 1964 - 1971.
WARWICK, Silas (2) Salford: 1907.
WATKINS, Billy (7) Salford: 1933 - 1937.
WATKINS, David (2+4) Salford: 1971 - 1974.
WATKINSON, David (12+1) Hull K.R.: 1979 - 1986.
WATSON, Cliff (29+1) St.Helens: 1963 - 1971.
WATTS, Basil (5) York: 1954 - 1955.
WEBSTER, Fred (3) Leeds: 1910.
WELLENS, Paul (16+2) St.Helens: 2001 - 2007.
WHITCOMBE, Frank (2) Bradford: 1946.
WHITE, Les (7) Hunslet: 1932 - 1933.
WHITE, Les (6) York & Wigan: 1946 - 1947.

DAVID HERON
Capped for Great Britain in 1982

WHITE, Tommy (3) Oldham: 1907.
WHITEHEAD, Derek (3) Warrington: 1971.
WHITELEY, Johnny (15) 1957 - 1962.
WILD, Stephen (1+1) Wigan & Huddersfield: 2004 - 2007.
WILKIN, Jon (1+3) St.Helens: 2007.
WILKINSON, Jack (11) Halifax & Wakefield: 1954 - 1962.
WILLIAMS, Billy (2) Salford: 1929 - 1932.
WILLIAMS, Dickie (12) Leeds & Hunslet: 1948 - 1954.
WILLIAMS, Frank (2) *R.D.* Halifax: 1914.
WILLIAMS, Peter (1+1) Salford: 1989.
WILLICOMBE, David (3) Halifax & Wigan: 1974.
WOOD, Alf (4) *R.D.* Oldham: 1911 - 1914.
WOODS, Harry (6) Liverpool Stanley & Leeds: 1936 - 1937.
WOODS, Jack (1) Barrow: 1933.
WOODS, John (7+4) Leigh & Warrington: 1979 - 1987.
WOODS, Tommy (2) Rochdale Hornets: 1911.
WORRALL, Mick (3) Oldham: 1984.
WRIGHT, Darren (+1) Widnes, 1988.
WRIGHT, Joe (1) Swinton: 1932.
WRIGHT, Stuart (7) Widnes: 1977 - 1978.
WRIGLESWORTH, Geoff (5) Leeds: 1965 - 1966.

Y

YEAMAN, Kirk (2) Hull: 2007.
YOUNG, Chris (5) Hull K.R.: 1967 - 1968.
YOUNG, Frank (1) Leeds: 1908.
YOUNG, Harold (1) Huddersfield: 1929.

GREAT BRITAIN INTERNATIONAL PLAYERS

(Pictured above) - The brilliant attacking style of DICKIE WILLIAMS for Great Britain as he slips a reverse pass to ERNEST WARD. Both were captains of Lions touring teams who also played in the internationals against France in the early 1950s.

They also played for Great Britain - in the years between 1952 and 1956 five full internationals were played between Great Britin and France. The British Rugby League authorities did not give full Test status to internationals against France until 1957, hence all the players who represented Great Britain in those games between 1952 and 1956 have never had their names recorded where they deserve to be, on the official register of Great Britain international players. On this page we list all those players and record their number of Great Britain appearances in the internationals against France pre-1957.

BANKS, Billy (2) Huddersfield.
BARTON, Frank (1) Wigan.
BEVAN, Dai (1) Wigan.
BOSTON, Billy (1) Wigan.
BOWDEN, Jim (1) Huddersfield.
BRIGGS, Brian (1) Huddersfield.
BROWN, Gordon (1) Leeds.
CAHILL, Ted (1) Rochdale Hornets.
CASTLE, Frank (2) Barrow.
CRACKNELL, Dick (1) Huddersfield.
DAVIES, Alan (2) Oldham.
EVANS, Jack (2) Hunslet.
FOSTER, Peter (1) Leigh.
FOX, Don (1) Featherstone Rovers.
GREENALL, Doug (2) St.Helens.
GRUNDY, Jack (1) Barrow.
HAYNES, Gordon (1) Swinton.
HOLLIDAY, Keith (1) Wakefield Trinity.
HORNE, Willie (1) Barrow.
IVISON, Billy (1) Workington Town.
JACKSON, Phil (2) Barrow.
JONES, Lewis (2) Leeds.
KELLY, Bob (1) Wakefield Trinity.
McCORMICK, Stan (1) St.Helens.

McKEOWN, John (1) Whitehaven.
McKINNEY, Tom (4) Salford & Warrington.
NAUGHTON, Alistair (2) Warrington.
PARSONS, George (1) St.Helens.
PAWSEY, Charlie (3) Leigh.
PRESCOTT, Alan (3) St.Helens.
PRICE, Ray (1) Belle Vue Rangers.
ROBINSON, Don (1) Leeds.
SCHOFIELD, Derrick (1) Halifax).
SILCOCK, Nat (1) Wigan.
SLEVIN, Ted (2) Huddersfield.
SMITH, Sam (1) Hunslet.
SOUTHWARD, Ike (1) Workington Town.
STEVENSON, Jeff (1) Leeds.
SULLIVAN, Mick (2) Huddersfield.
THORLEY, John (1) Halifax.
TOOHEY, Ted (1) Barrow.
TRAILL, Ken (1) Bradford Northern.
TURNBULL, Drew (1) Leeds.
VALENTINE, Dave (1) Huddersfield.
WARD, Ernest (1) Bradford Northern.
WILKINSON, Jack (1) Halifax.
WILLIAMS, Dickie (1) Hunslet.

TED SLEVIN - played in two internationals for Great Britain in his long and distinguished career.

SO - DID YOU KNOW?

ANSWERS TO THE QUIZ QUESTIONS IN OUR 'CLUB NOSTALGIA' PAGES

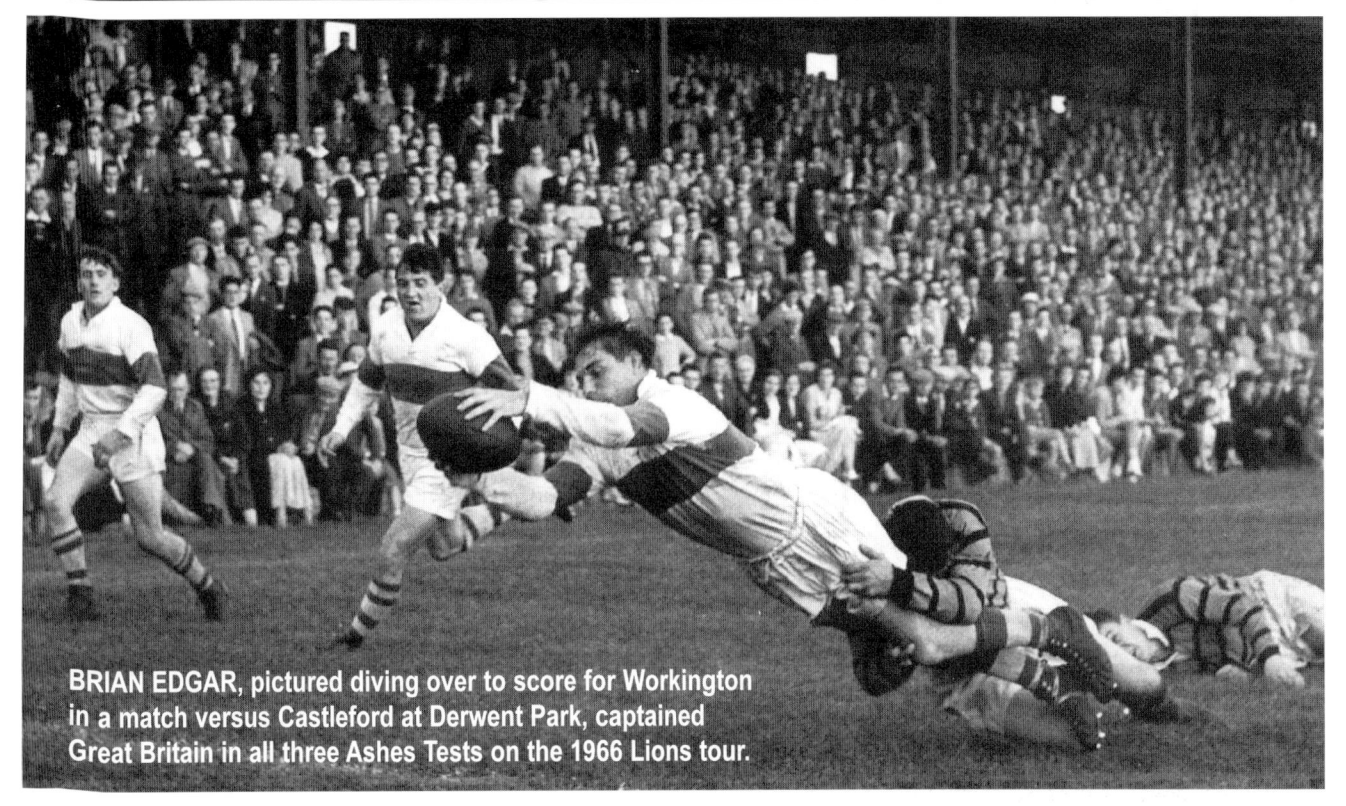

BRIAN EDGAR, pictured diving over to score for Workington in a match versus Castleford at Derwent Park, captained Great Britain in all three Ashes Tests on the 1966 Lions tour.

Barrow: Phil Hogan, with the 1977 Great Britain World Cup team.
Batley: Norman Field, who played on the wing in the 1963 first Test.
Blackpool: Howard "Smiler" Allen.
Bradford: Keith Mumby.
Bramley: John Wilson.
Castleford: Keith Howe, and his record was broken by St.John Ellis.
Dewsbury: Tommy Smales.
Doncaster: David Ellis.
Featherstone: Alan Agar, in 1983.
Halifax: Charlie Renilson.
Harlequins: Bradford Northern.
Huddersfield: Bob Nicholson.
Hull: Johnny Whiteley.
Hull Kingston Rovers: Frank Foster.
Hunslet: Brian Gabbitas.
Keighley: Phil Larder.
Leeds: Eric Harris, who had the nickname "The Toowoomba Ghost."
Leigh: Bev Risman.
Liverpool: Robin Whitfield.
Oldham: Bernard Ganley.
Rochdale Hornets: David Burke.
Salford: Lance B. Todd.
Sheffield Eagles: Alan Rhodes.
St.Helens: Bobbie Goulding.
Swinton: It was Rochdale.
Wakefeld Trinity: From Oldham.
Warrington: Bob Fulton.
Whitehaven: Vince Gribbin, in 1985.
Widnes: Doug Laughton.
Wigan: Graeme West, in 1985.
Workington Town: Brian Edgar.
York: Vic Yorke.

You can still enjoy our previous Annuals

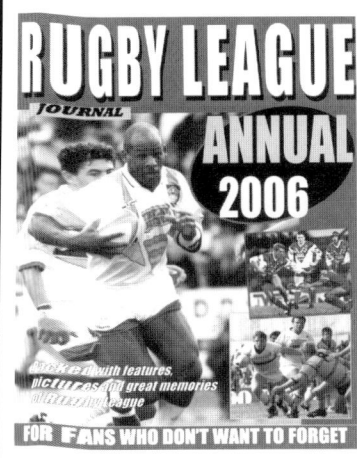

Have you just discovered our Annual with the book now in your hands, enjoyed it and would like more? You can still obtain copies of both our 2006 and 2007 Annuals, now each at the bargain price of only £9.95 (including postage) - *an effective saving of £5 per book.*
Both these Annuals are packed with a totally different selection of great Rugby League pictures and features - full of superb nostalgia.
To obtain either the 2006 or 2007 Annuals, just send cheque/P.O. for £9.95 per book
(payable to "Rugby League Journal") to:
Rugby League Journal, P.O.Box 22, Egremont, Cumbria, CA23 3WA.

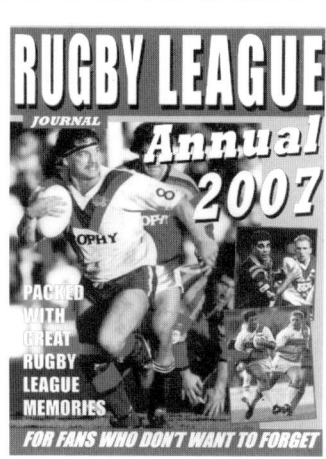

The FINAL WHISTLE

FEW sports can have changed as much as Rugby League. Always innovative and at the cutting edge of pushing back boundaries in the field of coaching analysis, training and player preparation, it has rarely got the credit it deserves for its courage and pioneering spirit. The list of Rugby League innovations is very long, be they from the use of floodlighting to substitutes; world cups to video referees; blood-bins to mini-rugby - Rugby League has led the way for other sports to follow. And, although much of the game may now look unrecognisable to many who remember it back in years gone by, the fundamentals remain the same of the skills and courage required to be able to play the game.

In the year 2007, the game bade farewell to one of its greatest champions of the modern era, with the retirement of the Kiwi Stacey Jones. His influence on the sport has been immense in the way he provided the guiding inspiration and driving force for two of its major attempts to create a professional presence in both New Zealand and France to take part alongside the established giants of Australia and Britain. In that department Stacey truly was an innovator - like he was with much of his play on the field (this is the man who invented the "banana kick" in rugby). And, in true Rugby League style, Stacey was the classic "little big man," further emphasising that in this game skill and intelligence will always triumph over physical bulk. It was a touching moment as Stacey played his farewell game for the Catalans before an adoring crowd in Perpignan, as he prepared to take a conversion as the last kick of the match, his little daughter brought the kicking-tee out for him. Stacey Jones will be badly missed by Rugby League.

Stacey Jones waves farewell.

And so will all the people who contributed so much to the game who have passed away since the last edition of this Annual came out. Among them: World Cup hero Jimmy Ledgard; Barrow's *"Indomitable"* Jimmy Lewthwaite; The French legend Gilbert Benausse; Great Britain internationals Peter "Flash" Flanagan, Berwyn Jones, Bill Martin and Jeff Stevenson - the last man to captain our country to win the Ashes on home soil - former Salford chairman Keith Snape and, our old friend the "Sergeant Major" Eric Clay, the game's most famous referee and the man who did so much to create the everlasting image of rugby referees being figures of respect. All those who gave so much to the game will never be forgotten.

If you have enjoyed this Annual, we are sure you will also enjoy our quarterly publication *"Rugby League Journal"* in which we regularly pay tribute to the people who shaped the history of the game. Here's wishing all of you good health and happiness in 2008, a year which will see several notable "anniversaries" for Rugby League which we will be acknowledging fully in the pages of our *"Journal."*
Happy Reading.
The Editor.

Additional copies of this Annual can be obtained by post from the address below, price £12.95 per book (post free.) Please pay by cheque/postal order made payable to "Rugby League Journal."

RUGBY LEAGUE JOURNAL
PUBLISHING

P.O. Box 22, Egremont, Cumbria, CA23 3WA
E-mail: rugbyleague.journal@virgin.net   Telephone: 01946 814249
www.rugbyleaguejournal.net